Symbol or Substance?

PETER KREEFT

Symbol or Substance?

A Dialogue on
the Eucharist with
C. S. Lewis,
J. R. R. Tolkien,
and Billy Graham

IGNATIUS PRESS   SAN FRANCISCO

Cover art and design by Enrique J. Aguilar

© 2019 Ignatius Press, San Francisco
All rights reserved
ISBN 978-1-62164-275-6
Library of Congress Control Number 2018949824
Printed in the United States of America ∞

Contents

Introduction 7

1. The Meeting 17

2. Is "Mere Christianity" a Mere Mirage? 23

3. Debating the Differences: The Agenda 37

4. Graham's Faith and Lewis' Critique 57

5. Lewis' Faith and Graham's Critique 69

6. Lewis' Faith Defended against Materialism
   and Magic 103

7. Other Possible Positions: Compromises? .. 129

8. Graham's Faith and Lewis' Deeper
   Critique 139

9. Tolkien vs. Lewis 161

10. Tolkien's Faith and Graham's Critique 175

11. Tolkien's Deeper Faith and Graham's
    Deeper Critique 203

12. Conclusions? 229

Introduction

The following conversation is fictional. It never happened, at least not in this world.

However, it very well could have. The idea of such a three-part conversation is not too far-fetched because two other conversations, which were the germs of my fictional one, actually did happen in this world.

(1) According to some sources, Lewis had a conversation with two people from the Billy Graham Evangelistic Association sent by Graham to Lewis to "feel him out"—an interview that sounds a little like the conversation between Jesus and the two messengers John the Baptist sent to Him when he was in prison (see Lk 7:19).

According to other sources, the visit was not from the Graham team but from Bob Jones, Jr., of Bob Jones University. I have assumed the first source rather than the second in this book, to make the conversation more intelligent, polite, and open-minded.

(2) Lewis also had very many conversations with his closest Roman Catholic friend, J. R. R. Tolkien; and at first some of these conversations were about their only serious difference of opinion, which was about Catholicism. Lewis had converted to Christianity with Tolkien's help, and Tolkien pressed him to take the next step, from Anglicanism to Catholicism.

Lewis was a man who loved controversy and argument as a bear loves honey; but he very uncharacteristically asked Tolkien to "cease and desist" from that one conversation topic for the sake of their continuing friendship, according to Christopher Derrick and Joseph Pearce, both of whom wrote books on why Lewis never "poped". Both report Lewis as saying to Tolkien something like: "You could not possibly understand where I am coming from; you were not born in Belfast."

So the literary genre of this book is neither simply fiction nor simply nonfiction. It is what C. S. Lewis called a "supposal" when pointing out that his Narnia books were neither allegories nor simple fantasies but imaginative answers to the question of what forms he supposes the Son of God might have taken and what actions He might have performed if He had become not only a man on earth but also a lion in another world (Narnia), a world of talking animals. Aslan is not an allegory for Jesus; Aslan *is* Jesus; that's what Lewis said to children who wrote to him that they were worried that they loved Aslan more than they loved Jesus.

Just as Aslan in Narnia is based on the historical figure of Jesus in this world, so my characters in this book (Lewis, Tolkien, and Billy Graham) are based on those three historical figures in this world. The difference between my "supposal" in this book and Lewis' in the Narnia books (besides the obvious one that the *Chronicles of Narnia* is a masterpiece) is that Lewis set his fiction in a world that was also fictional —he had the imagination to invent a whole fictional world—while I set mine in the real world, in Tolkien's home in Oxford.

I once wrote another imaginative "supposal" like this one, also in the form of a trialogue, a conversation among three famous people. In *Between Heaven and Hell*, I supposed that the three historical figures of C. S. Lewis, John F. Kennedy, and Aldous Huxley, all of whom died on the same afternoon of November 22, 1963, had a conversation about the meaning of life in general and the identity of Jesus in particular when they met in the next world after their nearly simultaneous deaths—a world that is neither fictional (like Narnia) nor historical (like Oxford). It "worked". It has been in print for thirty-five years and has sold over 100,000 copies. Like the conversation in this book, it *could* have happened.

I love to imagine three-way conversations among famous people. Another, shorter conversation I wrote was one with Lewis, Martin Luther, and Saint Thomas Aquinas. (That was part of *Ecumenical Jihad*.) Still another one was a series of dialogues among an Exclusivist, an Inclusivist, and a Pluralist at Harvard on the relations between the different religions of the world (*Between One Faith and Another*).

So in this book I picked three of the most famous, loved, and respected representatives of each of the three main Christian theological traditions or churches in the English-speaking world: the most famous modern Protestant evangelist (Billy Graham), the most famous modern Anglican Christian writer (C. S. Lewis), and the most famous and popular modern Roman Catholic writer (Tolkien), whose *The Lord*

of the Rings was picked by three reader polls as "the
greatest book of the twentieth century" and by another one as "the greatest book of the millennium".
Tolkien was not a religious apologist, preacher, or
theologian, but he called *The Lord of the Rings* "a
fundamentally Catholic and religious work".

I had the conversation move into many important
issues, as conversations naturally do, including some
of the classic differences between Protestants and
Catholics (faith and works, Bible and Church, tradition, authority, the pope). I had these three conver-
sationalists, however, concentrate on the Eucharist,
especially the Real Presence of Christ in it, because
broadening the conversation further to try to do even
a little justice to those other big issues would have re-
quired a book six times longer—and also because the
Eucharist was the most passionate issue in the great
divide of the Reformation, both between Catholics
and Protestants and even among different Protestants.
And naturally so, since the issue was nothing less than
whether Roman Catholics and "high Anglicans" or
"Anglo-Catholics" were committing idolatry in bowing to bread and worshipping wine, adoring a symbol that they mistook for the God it symbolized;
or whether Protestants were rejecting God's greatest gift, the most perfect, most intimate, most pow-
erful, and most complete union with their Lord that
was possible in this life, and reducing the substance,
the "real thing", to a mere symbol and/or a subjective experience. Anglicans took a *via media* position
on this, as on most issues, objecting to Rome's authority and insistence on Transubstantiation but af-
firming the Real Presence.

This is a great oversimplification, since during the Reformation there emerged a spectrum of quite a few different positions both among Protestants and among Anglicans, and there still are today. In fact, on this issue the difference between Anglicans and Baptists is far greater than the difference between Anglicans and Catholics.

A second reason why I focused on the Eucharist is that for me as a Roman Catholic the Eucharist is what it cannot be for a Protestant, viz., the source, summit, sum, and substance of my Christian life. But I also profoundly admire the faith, sanctity, sincerity, and personal passion of Billy Graham and also the mind of C. S. Lewis, who is clearly, in my opinion, the most brilliant and effective Christian writer of the last century.

Dearly would I love to have been a "fly on the wall" hearing a conversation among these three. But the only way I can hear it is to invent it first. I write the books that I wish someone else would write, but they don't, so I have to. If I'm to read them, I have to write them first. The same holds true for conversations.

I invite readers to be fellow flies on the wall listening to these three great Christians discuss one great mystery. (Of course, we would have to be invisible flies; if the three of them ever saw all of us on their wall, *they* would fly—out of the house and out of the conversation.)

Of all the words in this book, the chapter titles are the least important and the most misleading. I divided the conversation into short chapters merely as a convenience for readers' reference. You do not find such divisions in real conversations between friends, only in formal debates or medieval "scholastic disputations". Real conversations move like rivers, not like dominoes. I tried to depict the conversation as it would actually have happened, with all its twists and turns and tangents and repetitions.

Four Disclaimers

1. This is not a scholarly book. The pages of scholarship and theological argument about the Eucharist that have been published in the last five hundred years are long enough to reach to the moon if put end to end and heavy enough to sink a battleship if stacked top to bottom. Honest scholarship, even if it is partisan and polemical, is an honorable and necessary thing. But so is the exercise of common sense and basic logical reasoning, which ordinary people are perfectly capable of using, understanding, and evaluating. And so is imaginative fiction that concretizes and personalizes the great ideas and arguments for ordinary readers by putting them into the mouths of great characters in dramatic conversation.

2. I do not claim anything like the psychological and dramatic talents of a Plato, so at least two of my characters, Graham and Tolkien, do not always speak or act or feel exactly as their historical models did. My attempts to imitate their *style* of conversational speech is far from perfect, though I do claim it is accurate in terms of the *content* of their speech, of their beliefs. It is harder to imagine Graham and Tolkien in argument than Lewis because argument was not,

for them, as it was for Lewis, their primary or preferred mode of communication.

My Lewis character speaks more like Lewis, not only because I know Lewis better but also because he was more like me: unlike Graham or Tolkien, he was a philosopher. (After studying "Greats" at Oxford, he accepted a position in English literature only because there was no position open in philosophy.) The highest compliment anyone ever gave my writing was from George Sayer, Lewis' friend and biographer (he wrote the best biography of Lewis, *Jack*), when he asked me how many times I had met Lewis, and when I told him I had never met him, he said, "That's impossible. Your Lewis in *Between Heaven and Hell* matches not only the way he wrote but the way he talked." But I suspect that my other characters in this book talk too much like two other Lewises rather than themselves. I hope my readers judge that "one out of three ain't bad."

3. I try (in fact I demand of myself) to be not only as fair but also as sympathetic and understanding to the non-Catholic positions as I would hope a non-Catholic would be to the Catholic position. Nevertheless, because I am a Catholic, this book is and must be a book written by a Catholic, not by a Protestant or even a neutral agnostic. If a Protestant decided to write such a book, I would not expect it to be a Catholic book, only that the Catholic position be faithfully and fairly presented and argued for (and against).

I think I can do that to the Protestant position since I was an Evangelical Protestant (Reformed Church of America) for the first twenty-one years of my life and still have great admiration, respect, and love for the people and convictions of "the other side" (as should be clear in my recent book *Catholics and Protestants: What Can We Learn from Each Other?*). And I think I can do it to the Anglican position since (a) my favorite writer (Lewis) was an Anglican; (b) the congregation with which I worship is a Catholic "Anglican Use" congregation; and (c) the two greatest verbal achievements in the history of English-language Christianity are, to my mind, the King James Bible and the Anglican *Book of Common Prayer*.

4. I do not claim to have *settled* anything. Religion does not have "proofs" in the sense that science does. If you really want to know the truth, whether you are Catholic, Anglican, Protestant, Orthodox, "nondenominational", agnostic, or atheist, and whether you are wondering from the inside or from the outside, so to speak—that is, about your own position or that of others—in every case, you have one guaranteed method for finding out the truth for yourself (in God's time and in God's way, of course). That method is to pray. Pray with absolute, uncompromising, non-negotiable honesty, passion, and persistence. Ask the One who solemnly promised, "Seek and you shall find." He was talking, not about money or health or technology, but about truth, especially the truth about Him, which includes first of all the truth about who He is, but also, secondarily, about where He is and where we can find Him and whether or not He is really present hiding behind the sensory appearances in the Eucharist as well as living in our souls in what Mother Teresa called the "distressing

disguise" of the poor—which surely means, above all, the spiritually poor: ourselves.

You can pray even if you are an agnostic. Just be honest enough to tell God you doubt His existence but you're not absolutely certain, so you are making a sort of Pascal's Wager, addressing your prayer letter to "To Whom It May Concern" and mailing it to a house that you think is probably empty but just possibly may not be.

And even if you are an atheist, you can pray anyway if you are at all open-minded. (Unless, of course, you are infallibly and absolutely certain—but for that, don't you have to *be* God?) It's like a laboratory experiment to test a hypothesis. How do you test the hypothesis that there is a dead body buried in this yard? You don't just think, you dig. The man who claimed to be God incarnate solemnly promised that "all who seek, find." So to test that hypothesis, seek, question, ask, investigate. Dig. Dig deep. What are you afraid of? I know you don't believe in God, but He believes in you, and He has a great sense of humor. The two of you will have an uproarious laugh when you meet Him, in this world or in the next.

I think there is also a very fair and honest way for any Christian to test the very specific and astonishing Catholic claim that Christ is really present in the consecrated Host, wholly and personally and literally, Body and Blood, soul and divinity, hiding there behind the appearances of bread and wine as an angel usually hides behind what looks like a human body but that does not have a birth certificate or perhaps even a navel. (Next time you wonder whether you may be talking to an angel, ask his permission to look!) The way is very simple: Go into a Catholic church some time when no one is present to embarrass you or distract you, and pray: "Jesus, is that really You there in that little box on the altar under that red sanctuary lamp? If it is, oh, please, please draw me there. Feed me with Your Body and Blood, as You promised to do. If it is not You but only a symbol, then please, please do not draw me to this error. You are my only absolute; I want only to go wherever You are and not wherever You are not. The two last things I want to do are to commit idolatry and worship what is not You or to refuse to worship You where You really are. I do not want either to exalt the symbol into the substance or to reduce the substance to a symbol." Put the burden of your uncertainty on His shoulders, and let Him do the heavy lifting.

If you object to that method, I think you should first of all be reevaluating, not your Eucharistic theology, but your basic Christianity, your courage, and your honesty.

I

The Meeting

In my fictional scenario, during one of his evangelistic campaigns in England, Billy Graham had his private driver secretly take him to a prearranged meeting with Lewis at an inconspicuous rendezvous point, which was Tolkien's house in Oxford, where Lewis was waiting for him. Both Graham and Lewis invited the driver to come in and share the conversation. The driver's name was Guy, and he was a staunch Southern Baptist and a good friend and admirer of Billy's, though he thought Billy a bit too wishy-washy in his ecumenism and his welcoming attitude toward Catholics and Anglicans. I inserted him into the conversation to show a little of the dynamics and interchange among four positions, not just two or three.

At the door, GRAHAM greets Lewis with: "Doctor Livingstone, I presume?"

LEWIS [laughing heartily at the joke]: No, I'm only Lewis, not Livingstone; and you're only Billy, not Stanley, and this is only "darkest Oxford", not "darkest Africa".

GRAHAM: "Darkest Oxford"—that's a good one.

LEWIS: We used to send missionaries there, but now I think we should be asking them to send some here. I've never heard of an African atheist.

GRAHAM: I am very pleased to meet you, Doctor Lewis, even if you're not Doctor Livingstone. You are my brother in Christ. When I read your books, I feel your great faith and love for our common Lord and Savior. [He steps forward to give Lewis an American hug, which Lewis accepts with some surprise and embarrassment.]

LEWIS: And I am very pleased to meet you, too, sir. I profoundly admire what you do and what you have accomplished. And I honestly believe that in God's eyes you are one of His greatest warriors, while I am only a clerk, a scrivener. Our personalities are obviously very different, and so are our vocations—I am not a preacher or an evangelist but only what you would call an absentminded professor—but I believe we are fighting the same war, on the same battlefield, under the same Commanding Officer, and against the same enemies.

GRAHAM: That's a very fancy and flattering way of saying I am an evangelist and you are a theologian.

LEWIS: Not even a theologian. Not even a philosopher. Not an original one, anyway.

GRAHAM: An apologist, then.

LEWIS: Well, yes, both direct, in books like *Mere Christianity*, and indirect, in my fiction and in my literary essays.

TOLKIEN [from behind Lewis]: If you were both Catholics, you would probably be a Dominican, Jack, and Dr. Graham would be a Franciscan. You'd be Saint Thomas Aquinas, and he'd be Saint Bonaventure.

LEWIS [embarrassed a second time, turning around]: Oh, I'm so sorry, Tollers, I almost forgot whose house we were in. Dr. Graham, please meet our gracious host.

GRAHAM: Please call me Billy. We're friends here, not professionals.

TOLKIEN [also a little embarrassed]: Welcome, Dr. Graham—I mean friend Billy. Please excuse our English formality. And please know that any friend of Jack's is a friend of mine.

GRAHAM: And here is another friend, my driver, Guy. Thank you for inviting him, too.

GUY: I'm grateful to be in such famous company.

TOLKIEN: Here, don't stand in the doorway, come completely in, both of you, and sit down and have some tea and conversation.

GRAHAM: Don't mind if I do, thanks. By the way, I don't drink alcohol, but I have no objection to your drinking if you'd prefer that to tea.

TOLKIEN: No, tea will be fine for all of us. I think if it weren't for tea, the British Empire probably would have disappeared a long time ago. [They sit on dowdy old stuffed chairs around a coffee table in the unfashionable but not uncomfortable living room.] My family is away on vacation, all but my son Christopher here, who will be happy to serve you the tea. [Christopher appears, shakes hands, disappears, and reappears with tea and crumpets on a large tray a few minutes later. All take tea, but only Tolkien eats the crumpets; the other three are too fixated on the conversation.]

GRAHAM: Jack—may I call you Jack? [Lewis nods vigorously.] Thank you.—I think you will be amused by what my two spies told me about you when they visited you last month. I have read most of your books and admired them very much, but some of my staff were a bit suspicious of you. After they met you and I asked them about you, one of them said to me: "He smokes and he drinks and he swears, and yet I do believe he is a Christian!" [All have a hearty laugh.]

LEWIS: You probably have good reason to be suspicious of my piety, but not of my orthodoxy, I hope. At least it's not my intention to depart from the ancient apostolic faith.

GRAHAM: I'm not here as an agent of the Protestant Inquisition! I'm here to meet you, not to argue with you.

LEWIS: But I love argument! So I shall start one. I insist that what you do for our common faith is far more important and far more effective than what I do. When you arrive in Heaven, you will have a very long line of people waiting to thank you for being an instrument in their salvation. You fight like a great old warrior on the front line of the battlefield, while I sit behind the lines in comfortable barracks scribbling out books.

GRAHAM: But what books they are! I think your line for thank-you's will be longer than mine. *The Screwtape Letters* will be read a thousand years from now. The truths you tell there can never go out of date. And how tellingly you tell it! I could never begin to write that well.

LEWIS: And I could never begin to do what you do.

GRAHAM: What do you think I do?

LEWIS: You simply say, with your wonderfully simple heart, the wonderfully simple thing: "Come to Jesus." I am too proud and too private and too easily embarrassed to do that.

GRAHAM: I disagree. I think that is precisely what you do do, but indirectly, with your books. The Lord uses us in different ways because He gives us different talents. If I sow the seeds of the Gospel, you fertilize the fields, the minds of those I speak to; but as the Apostle Paul said, "I planted, Apollos watered, but it is God who gives the increase." He's the only One who gives life, who makes both the plants and the souls grow. I never converted anybody. It's only the Holy Spirit who does the converting.

LEWIS: That's true.

GRAHAM: So we are *both* wrong in our first little argument here: we shouldn't compare ourselves with each other, as we were both doing. All the power, and all the effective work in our souls and in our world, is God's work, not ours. So it's wrong for two of His fingers to argue about which one is the more important one or the less important one. I think that's what the Apostle Paul was trying to get across to the Corinthians when he wrote that.

LEWIS: I think you are absolutely right, Billy. You have won our first little argument.

GRAHAM: Here, look at the four of us here: two Evangelicals and a Roman Catholic and an Anglican, but with the same Lord. We're united in what you called *"Mere Christianity"*. And as you yourself said in that book, that thing—the thing that you called "mere Christianity"—isn't a set of ideas, a philosophy or an ideology or an *"ism"*—there's no such thing as "Christianism". It's a Person.

LEWIS: Yes, it is.

GRAHAM: Believe me, I'm not exaggerating here, Jack, and I'm certainly not trying to flatter you, but I honestly think that that modest little book of yours will do more for ecumenism, for unity among Christians, than any other book that's ever been written.

LEWIS [embarrassed]: Thank you.

GUY [interrupting]: I have a question to ask the two of you, if you don't mind.

Is "Mere Christianity"
a Mere Mirage?

GRAHAM: Of course we don't mind. You're here, too, Guy. You're not just my driver, you're a part of our conversation. What's your question?

GUY: Are you two really united? An Evangelical and an Anglo-Catholic? You disagree about some really important things—about the relation between the Bible and the Church and about the relation between faith and works and about devotion to saints and Mary and about Purgatory and the sacraments—how can you say you're united? Don't those differences matter?

LEWIS: Of course they matter. But I think our agreements matter even more, much more. Infinitely more. Because—as Billy just said and as I tried to put it in my preface to that book—what we have in common is not just some abstract "highest common factor", as we Brits say when we do maths. (I think you Americans call it a "lowest common denominator".) What unites us is not an idea or a set of ideas or our consensus about those ideas. It's a Person, a real Person, a divine Person.

GUY: And yet we do have serious disagreements, especially about that very Person, don't we? About His will for us and about what church is more faithful to Him?

GRAHAM: Unfortunately, yes. We can't deny that.

LEWIS: And you are right to be bothered by that, Guy. Profoundly right to be profoundly bothered.

GRAHAM: Both Jesus and Paul seem to have been profoundly bothered about it.

LEWIS: So what do you think we can do about it, Billy?

GRAHAM: We can start where you start, Jack: with "mere Christianity", not with Protestantism or Catholicism or Anglicanism. And we can spend more time and love and energy on that and less on our differences. For the very reason that you gave: because "that" is not an "it" but a "He".

TOLKIEN: Yes, that's all well and good, but I think there's a problem with that, Billy, and I think Jack does, too.

GRAHAM: What is the problem that you see there, Professor?

TOLKIEN: Oh, please call me Tollers, as Jack does. We're not in a classroom.

At this point Tolkien spills some tea, and Christopher comes in quickly to clean it up. When the conversation resumes, Lewis questions Tolkien:

LEWIS: Tollers, I'm a bit surprised by what you say. Why do you think *I* would have a problem with what

Billy said about "mere Christianity"? So far, I think what he said is the same thing as what I said.

TOLKIEN: Because of that "so far". It's not enough. And don't you think that can create a dangerous illusion?

LEWIS: What do you mean? What illusion?

TOLKIEN: As you yourself say in that very same book that Billy just praised so highly—here, let me read what you wrote in the introduction to that book, where you explain the title "Mere Christianity". Your book is here somewhere amid all this rubble, like a gold nugget in a big, dirty mine. [He goes to a messy bookcase and finds the book, which he opens, finds the page quickly, and reads:]

> I hope no reader will suppose that "mere" Christianity is here put forward as an alternative to the creeds of the existing communions—as if a man could adopt it in preference to Congregationalism or Greek Orthodoxy or anything else. It is more like a hall out of which doors open into several rooms. If I can bring anyone into that hall I shall have done what I attempted. But it is in the rooms, not in the hall, that there are fires and chairs and meals. The hall is a place to wait in, a place from which to try the various doors, not a place to live in.

GRAHAM: I think that is a very useful image, and a memorable one. And I agree with what you said, Tollers: It's not enough. It's a beginning—it's the necessary beginning—but it's just the beginning. You still have to pick and choose among the churches, which are unfortunately divided on some very important issues.

GUY: So how would you advise someone in the hall to choose which door to open, Doctor Lewis?

LEWIS: Oh, please, Guy, it's "Jack", not "Doctor Lewis", I'm not even a doctor, just a don.

GUY: Of course. Sorry.

LEWIS: I give my answer to your question in the next paragraph, I think. But if you don't mind, let me ask you first: How would *you* answer that question, Guy?

GUY: The Bible. It's what we all have in common. Go back to the Bible.

LEWIS: But we do. We all believe the Bible, as God's own Word to us. But we interpret it differently.

GUY: But it's our common data. The interpretations have to be judged by the data.

LEWIS: I agree. It's like science that way.

GUY: And all Christians believe that data, the Bible.

LEWIS: Yes, that's true. But all heretics in history have also appealed to the Bible.

GUY: Then stop adding the interpretations.

LEWIS: We don't *add* interpretations, like adding more books of the Bible: that would be heretical. But we have to interpret the books we have. You can't read any book without interpreting it.

GUY: Let the Bible interpret itself. "Interpreting Scripture by Scripture".

LEWIS: But the Bible can't interpret itself. No book can. The Bible is not a human being. It's a human being that has to interpret the data. *We* have to interpret the Bible.

GUY: All right, but we should interpret Scripture by Scripture, not by Tradition.

LEWIS: *Sola scriptura*, you say.

GUY: I do.

LEWIS: But that's precisely one of the biggest things that divide us. As a Reformation Protestant, you say *sola scriptura*; and, as a Roman Catholic, Tollers here says always to go by the Church's Sacred Tradition in interpreting the Bible because it's the only infallible interpretation; and we Anglicans take a *via media*, a middle way.

TOLKIEN: In fact, I'm almost as suspicious as Guy is of your "mere Christianity", Jack. It's an abstraction. The Church is a concrete thing, and she's been there for almost two thousand years, and Christ is her founder. If that's true, then we don't begin in any common hallway that you call "mere Christianity", as if it's a neutral starting point. The starting point is the Church Christ founded. Your "mere Christianity" presupposes the Reformation, presupposes the splitting of the seamless garment into different pieces of it. We're not equals. We Catholics came first. You're the rebels. You've broken off pieces of her, like limbs off a tree. You've cut the seamless garment into pieces, and now you're playing dice for the pieces.

GUY: What *you* see as the one thing is the Church, Tollers, and that's your unity, your solution to our disunity. But what we Protestants see as that one thing is the Bible. That's our unity and our solution. And you, Jack, you say there's a third answer, a middle position. But how can there be a *via media* between these two? One side claims that all other traditions, everything outside the Bible, is only human and fallible; and the other side claims that the Catholic Church's tradition is also divine revelation and infallible. How can there be a middle position between Yes and No to a church that claims it's infallible, or between Yes and No to *sola scriptura*?

LEWIS: That's a good question.

GUY: Do you have a good answer?

LEWIS: I think so. We Anglicans say that uniform Christian Tradition that comes from the Apostles and is taught by the consensus of all the Fathers of the Church, or almost all of them, has to be treated as authoritative, not just the bare Bible. Because it comes down to us from the Apostles and, thus, indirectly, from Christ. It's not just human opinions but part of divine revelation.

GUY: How do you Anglicans differ from Roman Catholics, then, about that "Sacred Tradition"?

LEWIS: For one thing, we don't restrict that to the Church of Rome. For another thing, we don't call the Church of Rome's dogmas or traditions or interpretations of Scripture "infallible". If we did, we'd have to discount the authority of our own church, our own English branch of Christendom, because Rome has decreed that our Anglican orders, our ordination of bishops, is invalid, that we have broken "apostolic succession". We don't believe we have done that. We believe we are a branch of the Church that is catholic, that is to say, universal.

GUY: So you see your church as having a different answer to the question of authority from that of either mine or Tolkien's—I mean Tollers'—different from either the Protestant or the Catholic answer.

LEWIS: Yes.

GRAHAM: Then what *is* your answer to Guy's question, Jack? How is somebody who has come into the common hallway of "mere Christianity" supposed to decide which room of the house to live in, which church or denomination to join?

LEWIS: The answer is right there in the same paragraph that Tollers just read. Here, let me find it. [Takes it from Tolkien and clumsily drops it, like a track and field runner dropping a baton. He picks it up and tries to find the passage. He is clumsy because he has only one working joint in his thumbs, not two; that was one reason he became a writer instead of anything more physical. Providence gave him a sub-par body and a super-par mind.]

GUY: But whatever your answer to that question is, it's got Lewis' fingerprints on it.

LEWIS: Of course. And so does your answer have your fingerprints on it. Neither of us denies the Bible, and neither of us can avoid interpreting it.

GUY: But my interpretation is also from the Bible.

LEWIS: But I claim that mine is, too.

GUY: But it isn't. Mine is simple and literal and adds nothing to the Bible. Yours is probably a lot more sophisticated and more scholarly and more intellectual than the average person's going to come up with. Your church is much less simple than mine. Mine is "Bible only", yours is "Bible plus". You have complexity; I have simplicity.

LEWIS: Guy, I think you will be surprised to discover that my answer to the difficult question of which church to join is not complex or sophisticated at all but very, very simple.

GUY: You think there's a simple answer to the question of what divides us? Of how to choose what church to join and how to choose what to believe?

LEWIS: I do.

GUY: What is it?

LEWIS: I think there can be only one honest reason why anyone should ever believe what any church teaches.

GUY [suspiciously]: What's that?

LEWIS: Because it's true.

GUY: Oh, yes, of course.

GRAHAM: I agree with that, too, Jack. But what about holiness? What about love? That has to count, too.

LEWIS: Yes, that too, but we have to ask whether it's *true* holiness and true love.

GUY: So your answer *is* simple. It's a one-word answer: Truth.

LEWIS: Yes. Here, I found the passage. [He reads it:] "Above all you must be asking which door is the true one; not which pleases you best. . . . The question should never be: 'Do I like that kind of service?' but 'Are these doctrines true? . . . Is my reluctance to knock at this door due to my pride, or my mere taste, or my personal dislike of this particular door-keeper?'"

GUY: So you say we have to start with "mere Christianity", but we can't stop there. We can't live in the hallway. We can't avoid the questions that divide the churches.

LEWIS: Not if we're honest truth seekers, no. That elephant is already in the living room. We can't ignore it.

GRAHAM: But don't you think we ought to pay less attention to our divisions and more to our common Lord?

LEWIS: I do, of course. We can't make our divisions primary or prior. But we can't ignore the elephant in our living room, either.

GRAHAM: I agree. Our divisions are indeed like an elephant, and I think we are too easily intimidated by it. I think a lot of the devil's strategy centers on the simple principle of "divide and conquer". So, Jack, how would you say we should balance our differences and our agreements?

LEWIS: I wholeheartedly agree with you that we have to begin with our agreements, because they direct our treatment of our disagreements. They include something very practical, like marching orders.

GUY: Are you saying that practice is more important than theology? That obedience is more important than truth?

LEWIS: No, because we need to know what orders are the true ones and what they mean. In that sense, knowing the truth has to come first, and then obedience. But in another sense, obedience has to come first: we have to obey the command to be honest and to seek the truth. So each is prior and absolute, because each depends on the other.

GUY: That's a good answer to a tough question.

LEWIS: It's more than just a good answer, it's a practical necessity, because we are not just arguing about ideas; we are on a dangerous battlefield.

GUY: You mean the wars of religion ever since the Reformation?

LEWIS: No, I'm speaking of a far more important war than that.

GUY: What do you mean?

LEWIS: I mean the war that started with a snake and an apple in a garden.

GUY: Oh. Yes. That is indeed a bigger battlefield. That changed everything.

LEWIS: And so did the invasion.

GUY: The invasion?

LEWIS: The Incarnation. Remember what He said in John's vision in Revelation? "Behold, I make all things new."

GRAHAM: You're right, Jack. The three most important events in history, the three that change *everything*, are the Fall, the Incarnation, and the Second Coming.

LEWIS: So now for the rest of time we live during the great world war that's the plot of all of the rest of history, all the time between those last two events, His two comings. We have to put our divisions into that perspective. They're civil wars, and the devil loves them and inspires them because he knows the most obvious principle of military strategy: "divide and conquer." That's why it's so important never to forget that we're all on a common mission from our common Commanding Officer. His words are not just good advice for happy living or abstract truths to satisfy our philosophical curiosity, but life or death marching orders.

GRAHAM: That is my vision of life, too, Jack.

GUY: And the Bible is our marching orders. But we interpret them differently. That's why we fight our civil wars, especially the one between Protestants and Catholics.

GRAHAM: We may differ about how we interpret His orders, but we don't differ about who our Commander is or about our absolute loyalty to Him.

GUY: I think we all agree about that. But how does that answer the questions that divide us?

LEWIS: Well, first of all, it means that we should do what we're doing now when we talk about those questions. We dare not forget the "big picture", as I think you Americans say. We can't ignore our civil wars, but we have to frame them by our common world war, so to speak, the war against the "principalities and powers of wickedness".

GRAHAM: And that "big picture" is what you call "mere Christianity".

LEWIS: Yes. But then there's also a second thing, which I think is just as necessary: we can't ignore our differences any more than we can forget our agreements, even if our agreements are much more important than our differences. We can't paper them over —you can't paper over an elephant.

GRAHAM: Jack, you said in the preface to *Mere Christianity* that you thought God had put you on the area of the battlefield that was most central but that was also the most poorly defended, the common teachings of "mere Christianity". That's fine, and terribly necessary, and I think all Christians have to be deeply grateful to you for that book. But why isn't that papering over the elephant? Where do you confront the elephant?

GUY: In other words, do you practice what you preach?

At this point Tolkien, who has been silent, sits up to sudden attention and nods vigorously. He opens his mouth to reinforce Graham's and Guy's question, but quickly closes it, deciding that it is too personal. Also, and for friendship's sake, he does not want to "gang up on" Lewis.

LEWIS: I do try to practice what I preach about the elephant. You may be surprised to hear this, but, a Roman Catholic priest in Italy and I send each other a letter every year, in Latin, about exactly that problem, about ecumenism, about the problem of our disunity, which we both agonize over, as Saint Paul did in the beginning of First Corinthians and as Our Lord did in His "high priestly prayer" in John 17. We both pray what Christ prayed for all His disciples, "that they may be one", but we don't know how to make them one.[1]

TOLKIEN [chafing at the bit]: *I do!* [All heads turn, surprised.] There is a very simple and concrete answer to that question. Come home, children, come home.

LEWIS: Of course you Catholics think you have the answer, but that's exactly what we disagree about.

GRAHAM: But even though you two disagree about the claims of the Roman Church, you agree that your disagreements are disagreeable.

LEWIS and TOLKIEN together: Exactly.

---

[1] These letters, a model of an ecumenical dialogue that is mutually respectful yet not compromising, have been published as *The Latin Letters of C. S. Lewis*. (They are available either in English only or in the original Latin with the English translation on facing pages.) Lewis' correspondent, Dom Giovanni Calabria, was canonized as a saint by Pope Saint John Paul II. The Catholic Church has not gotten around to canonizing any non-Catholics yet; but when she does, I suspect that Graham and Lewis may be two of the first.

GUY: But that's not enough! Honestly, guys, I have to register a disappointment here. [The others are surprised. Guy explains:] I was really, really grateful to be invited to this conversation, since I'm not a writer, not an intellectual, and not at all famous, as all three of you are. But I thought I was going to hear a debate, and instead I seem to be hearing an ecumenical love fest.

GRAHAM: Is that a bad thing?

GUY: No, of course not, that's great—love is great, especially among Christians. Of course. But . . .

GRAHAM: I don't think it *is* an "of course". I think it's one of the most demanding tasks in the world. And I think our lack of love for each other was the first cause of our divisions. Do you think that if we were all saints we would have the disagreements and divisions that we have now?

GUY: I guess not. But we're not all saints, and we still have those divisions and disagreements, and I was hoping I'd hear a debate about them between two or three of my favorite people in the world, on the most important subject in the world, religious truth, and I'm going to be disappointed if I can't hear that. So I have to ask you now: Are we going to debate our differences or not?

3

Debating the Differences:
The Agenda

GRAHAM: I'm not a debater, Guy, just an evangelist. And I didn't come here for a debate; I came for a friendly conversation.

GUY: But Billy, I've never known you to avoid a good, honest question.

GRAHAM: I admit that. I will answer—I will *try* to answer—any sincere question anyone ever asks me, if I can. But Guy, I came here to listen—to listen to two great men and great minds and great writers —and, more importantly, also great Christians, who love the same Lord as I do; but both of them have a somewhat different set of beliefs than I do about Him, or at least about His church. I'm perfectly willing to have a friendly and respectful debate about our differences, if you all want to do that, but first of all I want to listen, to try to understand where these two men are coming from, what they believe and why they believe it. So I think I'm not being evasive, Guy.

GUY: Oh, I didn't mean to imply that you were, not at all.

LEWIS: And I welcomed you here, not to a debate, but to a friendly conversation, Billy. And, like you, I'm also interested in listening first of all—listening to you, because you have a gift from God that I simply do not have. But I must confess I also love a good argument between friends. We do that every week in our Inklings meetings, and not just then but any time we feel like it, over dinner or at a pub or while we're out walking through the country, which we do a lot. Food and drink and walking and conversation and friendship—those have to be five of the greatest things in the world. And when it comes to conversation, neither of us likes "small talk" and both of us love to argue.

GUY: Good! Because even if we call it a conversation instead of a debate or an argument, we have here three Christians who have serious disagreements, and I hope we can explore those, and I hope you can explain to me and to each other just what you believe and why you believe what you believe, and why you two disagree with each other about some things and with some of the things Billy believes. We're not going to tiptoe around our disagreements, are we?

LEWIS: I hope not. By the way, we are four Christians here, not three, Guy. You count just as much as we do.

GUY: Thanks, Jack.

LEWIS: So is it agreed to disagree together?

ALL: Yes.

LEWIS: Are you in, too, Tollers?

TOLKIEN: Of course I am. Need you ask?

LEWIS: You've been as silent as a rock.

TOLKIEN: Like the rock of Saint Peter, I hope. As the only Roman Catholic here, I shall stand on that rock, and I shall be happy to try to defend it, but only as a very amateurish theologian. Thank God, it certainly wasn't on me that Our Lord promised to build His Church.

LEWIS: So we will do what you and I both want, Guy: we will have a debate as well as a listening. Both, of course, since you can't honestly debate unless you first honestly listen.

GUY: Thanks, guys. As long as Billy has no objections.

GRAHAM: Not only do I have no objections, but I'm eager to do that. I think Christians make the best debaters.

LEWIS: Why?

GRAHAM: Because when we debate, we do it as we do everything else, under obedience—obedience to Christ's two absolutes: truth and love. And that means total honesty *and* total respect.

LEWIS: Touché!

GRAHAM: I take it that's the British version of "amen".

LEWIS: It's French for a "touch"—a point in fencing. I think the American version is "Gotcha!" We Brits try to be polite instead of enthusiastic.

TOLKIEN: Billy, would you like to hear our definition of Heaven and Hell?

GRAHAM: Go ahead.

TOLKIEN: In Heaven everyone is as polite as an Englishman and as enthusiastic as an American. In Hell everyone is as polite as an American and as enthusiastic as an Englishman.

GRAHAM: Hmmm . . . Guy, do you think we're being insulted or complimented?

GUY: I think we're being touché-ed. But to get down to business, if I may ask the three of you the crucial question: What do you think is the most important disagreement you have?

LEWIS: Of course you may ask. It's a good question.

TOLKIEN: I'm not sure what the right answer to that question is, but I think it has to be something very specific and concrete, not something general and abstract, like "What is the true religion?" or "What is the true Church?" People fight wars over specific issues, not over generalities. Soldiers sacrifice their lives for their buddies; life for life, not for abstractions.

GRAHAM: So what *is* the issue that divides us the most?

LEWIS: I think I know enough about the history of the Reformation to answer that question. What question do both sides think the other side was not just wrong about but on the devil's side about?

GRAHAM: You said you thought you knew the answer from history, Jack. What is it?

LEWIS: I think it was two things. One was the pope's claims to be the universal Vicar of Christ, to have divine authority over all Christians—and, associated with that, the Church's claims to temporal and political power. Sometimes even total power. Remember Pope Gelasius I's theory of "the two swords", temporal and eternal, spiritual and political. And remember the Spanish Inquisition. Many Protestants went so far as to call the pope the Antichrist. The other was the Church's doctrine of what happens in the Mass, in the Eucharist. Is that worship or idolatry? Is Christ really present there, or is it just bread and wine, a holy symbol?

TOLKIEN: As the only Roman Catholic here, I agree with that. Those were the two most fiery issues.

GRAHAM: Wasn't it justification by faith? Luther did not want to start a new church, but he was convinced that Catholics just didn't know how to get to Heaven.

LEWIS: Among the theologians, yes, that was the number one issue, especially among Lutherans. But not, I think, among ordinary people.

GUY: So do you want to debate the pope's authority? Or the political authority of the Church?

LEWIS: No . . .

GUY: Because you don't want us three to gang up on Tollers?

LEWIS: No . . .

GUY: Because you want to broaden the issue to Church and state, or religion and politics?

LEWIS: No. Because I don't think that issue is the one we ought to be arguing about today anymore.

GUY: Why not?

LEWIS: Because, like everything political, the relation between the Church and the state have changed
so much throughout history, and so have the visible forms of authority within the Church. At first,
the bishop of Rome was simply the court of final ap-
peal . . .

TOLKIEN: "Rome has spoken, the case is closed."

LEWIS: Yes, that was an early formula. But after Con-
stantine and during the Middle Ages, the Church became much stronger politically, and she claimed more
and more political power, and she got it, before she
was divided in 1054 and then again in 1517, and again
and again after that. And that diminished her power.
And her *claims* to political power. The Church has
divested herself of most of her temporal or secular
political power in modern times, so that's not the
major issue anymore.

GUY: You mean it was taken from her. She didn't will-
ingly abdicate. "The Glorious Revolution" had to be
fought on the battlefield, not just in the seminaries.
And it had casualties. And if it hadn't been for the
carnage of the Thirty Years' War, the Church never
would have agreed to the separation of Church and
state in the Peace of Westphalia.

TOLKIEN: That may be true, but she's not claiming
political power today. So we would be beating a dead
horse if we argued about what she should have done
in the past. And she never did claim political power
infallibly or dogmatically. Only her dogmas are unchangeable, not her politics.

GUY: She still has Vatican City as a sovereign state.

TOLKIEN: Only for independence, to be left alone, not for any temporal ambitions of her own. The Swiss Guards are not going to start a war against Italy tomorrow to restore the Papal States!

GRAHAM: I think you two are right, then, when you say that the political issue is not something to argue about anymore. The past is past. Why keep fighting wars that have ended?

GUY: But the authority of the pope is not a political issue. It's a religious issue. And it still divides us.

GRAHAM: Yes, it is, and it does. But I don't think it's the deepest one.

GUY: Why not?

GRAHAM: Because it's not spiritual, it's *administrative*. The administrative is relative, the spiritual is absolute.

GUY: What do you mean by that?

GRAHAM: Well, administration is about temporal, visible power and organization, like politics, even when what is administrated is a church; but religion is about eternal truth and eternal salvation. Temporal power is relative, but eternal truth is absolute. So for me, the issue of the pope's authority is relative to the issue of what he teaches. If the pope taught everything we Reformation Protestants teach, if he saw himself simply as the servant of the Bible, then I don't think we'd have that much of a problem with him, any more than you Anglicans have problems with the primacy of the archbishop of Canterbury. Do you agree with that, Guy?

GUY: I guess I do.

GRAHAM: But you don't, right, Tollers?

TOLKIEN: No. We Catholics don't limit the pope's authority to teaching the Bible. That would mean he'd have less authority than you do if you taught more of the Bible or taught it better than he did. No, we believe the popes are the successors of Saint Peter, to whom Christ entrusted, personally and by name, the keys of the Kingdom of Heaven. But we have no divinely revealed and unchangeable dogma about the extent of the pope's temporal power, or even about the order inside the Church, for instance, about how popes and bishops are to be selected. That has changed throughout our history.

GRAHAM: So that's a non-issue.

GUY: But, Tollers, I think you'd like to turn back the clock to before the Glorious Revolution and to before the Peace of Westphalia, wouldn't you, to before the separation of Church and state? I've always thought of that as a Protestant principle, and I don't think Catholics are quite happy with it.

TOLKIEN: You're wrong. As a Catholic, I have nothing against it. In fact, I think it's a very healthy principle.

GUY: Because it keeps the state from being corrupted by the Church and her lust for religious power?

TOLKIEN: No, because it keeps the Church from being corrupted by the state and its lust for political power.

LEWIS: I agree with Tollers. I don't think the separation of Church and state is an absolute, so even if it did divide some of us, even if some Catholics longed for a restoration of the Middle Ages, it doesn't divide us all and it doesn't divide us *passionately*. It's not a dogma, so neither side should be dogmatic about it. We're not going to go to war about relativities.

GUY: Are you saying that truth in politics is relative?

LEWIS: No, there are some bedrock moral principles there. But (as I pointed out in *Mere Christianity*) Christianity has never insisted on any one political system, unlike Islam, which claims the authority of divine revelation for theirs, and unlike Old Testament Judaism, which actually had one for a while. The New Testament gives you a few foundational moral principles for politics, but not a political system. For instance, it neither approves nor condemns either monarchy or aristocracy or democracy, or a blend of all three, which is what Thomas Aquinas thought was the best government.

GRAHAM: Do you personally agree with him, by the way?

LEWIS: Yes, and also with Hooker. But I think that kind of balance is the hardest to maintain, and the hardest to define, and also the most flexible and relative.

GUY: How is it relative?

LEWIS: What's relative is what forms it should take and how much of each of those three ingredients there should be.

GRAHAM: But the Bible does give us some important spiritual principles for politics.

LEWIS: Indeed. But its principles don't fit any of our present political alternatives. Its emphasis on hierarchy and authority and obedience offends the Left, and its emphasis on equality and community and on sharing property and on charity to the poor offends the Right.

So I don't think we can profitably focus on that issue. It no longer divides us *religiously*—unless we make politics our end and religion our means, which is idolatry.

GRAHAM: You mentioned *two* issues, Jack, so if we leave the first one alone, that leaves the second one, which was the Eucharist.

TOLKIEN: And I think we can all see why it's so divisive. If we Catholics are right, you Protestants are missing out on more than a holy symbol; it's Christ Himself.

GRAHAM: Do you mean that you Catholics believe that we Protestants can't have Christ in our souls and be saved if we don't partake of your Catholic sacraments?

TOLKIEN: No, no, not at all.

GRAHAM: What do you mean, then? What are we missing if we have Christ?

TOLKIEN: You are missing out on the most total and complete and perfect union with Christ that is given to man in this world, in this life. If I may dare to use the image that the great mystics use, beginning with the Song of Songs, your Protestant religion is like a marriage without intercourse. Religion is a kind of spiritual marriage between God and man, and the Eucharist is spiritual union between the two spouses, a union of bodies as well as souls, though of course it's not sexual and biological.

GUY: But if you're wrong about that, then you're idolaters. You're bowing to bread with awe and dread and worshipping wine as if it's divine!

LEWIS [laughing]: That's good doggerel, but bad theology. Is that a quote from one of your anti-Catholic hymns?

GUY [surprised and a bit offended]: No, of course not.

LEWIS: I was only—what do you say? Kidding, not serious.

GUY: But seriously, that *is* a serious mistake. In fact, it's an even *more* serious mistake than the one you say we Protestants are making. It's disobeying what Christ called "the first and greatest commandment"!

LEWIS: That's why that issue is so volatile.

GRAHAM: And where do you stand on that, Jack? What do you believe about the Eucharist, the Mass, the sacred liturgy, Holy Communion, or the sacrament of the Lord's Supper? We all call it by different names. Is it more than a symbol?

LEWIS: Yes. For most of you Protestants, it's a symbol of Christ; for us Anglicans as well as Roman Catholics, it's the substance of Christ.

GRAHAM: What do you mean by that?

LEWIS: To be quite honest with you, I don't know *exactly*, and I don't know if anybody does. I've never been fond of the term "substance", or the Roman explanation of "transubstantiation". "Real Presence" is enough for me. For me it's not the theological explanation that counts; it's the reality of Christ. He is really there, to be adored.

GUY: So do you say to that little piece of bread what Doubting Thomas said to Christ? "My Lord and my God"?

LEWIS: That is exactly what I say. Because it's *not* bread. It's Him.

GRAHAM: That's what your church teaches, as well as the Roman Catholic Church, right?

LEWIS: We agree with Rome on the Real Presence of Christ in the Sacrament, yes.

GRAHAM: We Protestants celebrate the Lord's Supper, too. How do you see us as Protestants and what we do when we celebrate that sacrament? What is your theology about that? What do you think we have, and what do you think we lack?

LEWIS: I'm sorry to disappoint you, but, as I said before, I am not a theologian. I'm just an ordinary, believing layman of the Church of England, and I don't have anything original to teach about that. I'm not a cleric, just a clerk. I believe my own church's position, which seems to me to be a reasonable and moderate middle position between the Protestant one and the Catholic one.

GUY: How? It seems much closer to the Catholic position to me.

LEWIS: Oh, it is, on the issue of the Real Presence. But I don't believe in the Catholic (and Eastern Orthodox) claim to possess the only valid Eucharist. If you want to put it in negative terms, I think the Catholics claim too much and the Protestants claim too little.

TOLKIEN: But if you agree with us Catholics and not the Protestants about the Real Presence of Christ in the Sacrament, then you're on our side on that single central issue that most divides us. Even if you disagree with us both, you disagree more with them than you do with us. You see our Catholic "too much" as only a little too much and the Protestants' "too little" as a lot too little.

LEWIS: I'm suspicious of putting it in quantitative terms, "more" or "less".

TOLKIEN: But you agree that the Protestants believe too little.

LEWIS: On this issue, yes, of course.

GRAHAM: Jack, can you tell me a little more clearly why you think we Protestants believe too little? What do you think we *do* believe about the Lord's Supper?

LEWIS: That it's only a holy symbol of Christ, not the substance of Christ. Isn't that the classical Protestant position, Billy?

GRAHAM: I wouldn't say that, no. That's too simple. I wouldn't reduce it to that.

GUY: *I* would.

LEWIS: Hmmm. It looks like we have not just two positions, as the Catholics say—theirs and all denials of theirs—or even just three, as I said, adding the Anglican *via media*, but *four* positions.

TOLKIEN: Actually, there were more than four different positions in the Reformation debate, if I remember my history.

GRAHAM: Can you sort that out for us, Tollers?

TOLKIEN: I'll try. Let's see. First, there was the Catholic position, which had been around from the beginning and which came to be defined as Transubstantiation by the Council of Trent. Then there was Luther's position, which was Consubstantiation instead of Transubstantiation—Luther claimed that Christ is really present but *along with* the bread and wine; the bread and wine remain bread and wine. Third came Zwingli's position, which denied the Real Presence and said it's only a symbol. I think that's where you stand, Guy, if I'm not mistaken. Fourth came Calvin, who tried to reconcile Luther and Zwingli, but, instead of doing that, he created a fourth position that contradicted both. He denied Christ's Real Presence in the Sacrament, but he said it was "a sign and a seal", which is more than just a symbol. And now I think we're hearing a fifth position from you, Billy, somewhere between Zwingli and Calvin, if I'm not mistaken.

GRAHAM: You *are* mistaken. I'm not staking out a new position or an old one. I don't want to pinpoint my position on that theological spectrum. My point is not which theologian I say is closest to the truth; my point is that we ought to focus on the bigger picture, on the Christ we all believe in as our Lord and our Savior; and I think our differences will become much less important if we take that perspective.

TOLKIEN: That wasn't Luther's position *or* Zwingli's. Luther wrote something like this: "We have here two ideas, and one of them is from God and the other one is from the devil. And I do not get my ideas from the devil."

GRAHAM: Well, I certainly disagree with Luther there. I don't demonize anybody.

TOLKIEN: Fine. But that doesn't solve the problem. Either Christ is really present there, or He is not. What do you say about that? Which is the truth there?

GRAHAM: The truth is that Christ does not want His disciples to call each other devils! He wants us to love each other.

TOLKIEN: Yes, of course He does, but that still doesn't tell us what is true. Surely you're not ignoring that question or reducing objective truth to subjective sincerity?

GRAHAM: Certainly not. But I believe that the only truths about God of which we can be absolutely certain are the truths in Scripture.

TOLKIEN: But how do you know what these truths in Scripture mean? You have to interpret them. How did the early Christians know that God was a Trinity of three equally divine Persons? The Bible doesn't directly address that question. It never uses the word "Trinity".

GRAHAM: It gives us all the data we need: that there is only one God, that the Father is God, that the Son is God, that the Holy Spirit is God, and that the Father and the Son and the Holy Spirit are different Persons.

TOLKIEN: But the heretics believed that biblical data, too. The only reason we know they were wrong is that the Church labeled them wrong and defined the truth in creeds. It took hundreds of years. It wasn't easy. It was like science: all scientists accept the data, but it takes a lot of collective effort to arrive at the truth that does justice to all the data and to express it in a universal formula like force equaling mass times acceleration or gravity being relative to mass and distance —whatever the mathematical formula is—and energy equaling mass times the speed of light squared. If the Church had let each individual interpret the Scriptures in his own way, we would never have the doctrine of the Trinity, and eventually we'd have as many different churches as there are Christians.

GRAHAM: My religion isn't based on my theology of the Trinity; it's based on the Person of Christ.

TOLKIEN: But how do you know that Christ isn't just an appearance and not really a human being, as the Docetist and Gnostic heretics said? And how do you know He's not just the first and best creature, as the Arian heretics said, or just "the man for others", as modernists say? How do you know He is fully human and fully divine at the same time, one Person with two natures? The Bible never directly says that.

GRAHAM: All orthodox Christians believe it.

TOLKIEN: But it's the Church that defined orthodoxy. And she had to, because half the Christians in the world denied His full divinity for over a century, in the Arian heresy. And there are still plenty of people today who call themselves Christians who are "liberals" or "modernists" who deny His divinity and deny the supernatural altogether.

GRAHAM: Scripture refutes them. "Jesus is Lord"— that's in Scripture. That's the first creed, and the most fundamental one. And "Lord"—*kyrios*—always meant God, not any human lord, in the Christian's vocabulary.

TOLKIEN: The heretics accepted that, too, but they interpreted it differently. You can't ignore history, Billy. It's simply a historical fact that the only way Christians knew how to interpret the Bible, on the two doctrines that defined the Christian religion, the Trinity and the nature of Christ, was through the authority of the Church. That's why Christ gave us the Church. He didn't write the Bible; He established the Church. That's a historical fact.

And it's also a historical fact that the only way we know which books are part of the Bible is because the Church defined the canon of sacred books. Luther thought the Epistle of James was not part of the Bible because it says that we are not justified by faith alone but also by works. How do you know he's wrong?

GRAHAM: Oh, I agree with the need for the Church —because that's in the Bible, too! But I will not add anything to the Bible. The Bible tells us everything we need to know for our salvation. And the Bible says, in almost its last verse, "Cursed be anyone who adds to the words of this prophecy." You Catholics add Tradition to Scripture; we Protestants don't.

TOLKIEN: But here is another historical fact that you can't deny: Scripture didn't come first; Sacred Tradition did. The Gospel was preached orally long before it was put in a book. According to the Bible, Christ commanded His disciples to preach, not to write. And when they wrote, they wrote what they had first preached.

GRAHAM: So you Catholics put Tradition first.

TOLKIEN: First in time, yes. It *came* first in time. That's one of those historical facts. And first in causality, too, because the Bible was written by the Church; the New Testament was written by the Apostles and their disciples. But not first in authority: we accept both Scripture and Tradition—not human traditions, not man-made traditions, like the rules about fasting —those are fallible and changeable—but the Sacred Tradition that comes from Christ and the Apostles. That's what Scripture appeals to, too; Saint Paul is always appealing to Tradition in his letters. The only Scripture he appealed to was the Old Testament because that was the only Scripture his readers had so far. Another historical fact.

GUY: Tollers, I think this argument is a little unfair. You're playing the game on your playing field, not Billy's. Billy doesn't claim to be a historian or a theologian. We've got plenty of those, just as you do, and I think they could give you a run for your money if they were here.

LEWIS: Perhaps so, but I think we're digressing. The historical issues are important, of course, and especially what kind of authority historical tradition has. (I take a position somewhere between the two of you there.) But we're supposed to be focusing on the Eucharist, aren't we? Wasn't that our agenda?

ALL: Yes.

LEWIS: So I'd like to hear more from Billy about just what he believes about that, because I don't think I understand it well enough to argue about it. I think I understand the classic positions, including three versions of the Real Presence, the Roman, the Lutheran, and the Anglican, and I understand the position that says it's just a symbol—that's Zwingli, and Guy, too —but I don't know Calvin's position very well, and Billy, I think your position sounds like something that's somewhere between those two, Calvin's and Zwingli's. But I don't understand how there can be a third position between Real Presence and Only Symbolic Presence. Could you tell me just what you believe about the Eucharist?

GRAHAM: I'm not a theologian, either, but I can tell you what I believe.

*At this point, Christopher came in to pour more hot wa-
ter into their teapot, which had gotten cold because the conversation had claimed all their attention. So the four took a
short tea break. When they resumed, Graham began again.*

4

Graham's Faith
and Lewis' Critique

GRAHAM: Let me try to explain my convictions about what I call the Lord's Supper and you call the Eucharist. I have serious reservations about the Catholic theology of the Mass as a sacrifice, but I'd rather not get into that now.

GUY: Because it's too personal and prickly and passionate?

GRAHAM: No, because it's too technical, too theological. I want to concentrate on what I think we all saw as the specific issue that divides us most seriously and most clearly: Is that thing which looks like bread and wine really the Body and Blood of Our Lord and is thus to be worshipped, or is it only a holy symbol to be respected but not Christ Himself and not to be worshipped? How is Christ present in Holy Communion? Are we Protestants reducing Christ there to bread, or are you Catholics worshipping bread as if it were Christ? As you pointed out, Jack, that's the issue that most passionately sparked many of the wars of religion after the Reformation. And we can see why.

LEWIS: So can you tell us what you believe about that sacrament? I want to see how it differs from what Tollers and I believe and also from what Guy believes. I suspect you're closer to Calvin and he's closer to Zwingli.

GRAHAM: Let's start with my public statement about it. Guy, do you have those questions and answers with you? The ones that our ministry is going to publish?

GUY: Yes, I do, right here in this briefcase.

GRAHAM: May I see them? Thanks. Here it is. Here is what I recently replied to someone who was asking the question you are asking me. [He reads it.]

The question was this: "The church we started attending several months ago places a lot more emphasis on observing the Lord's Supper than our previous church did. Does the Bible say much about the Lord's Supper and how we ought to observe it?"

And here is the answer I gave:

While churches differ in their understanding of the Lord's Supper (or, as some churches call it, Communion or the Eucharist), they all realize its importance and seek to give it a central place in their worship. This has been true since the beginning of the Christian faith.

The reason is simple: Jesus told His disciples to celebrate it regularly until He comes again, just as He celebrated it with them shortly before His death. The Apostle Paul recorded that first Lord's Supper this way: "The Lord Jesus, on the night he was betrayed, took bread, and when he had given thanks, he broke it and said,

'This is my body, which is for you; do this in re-
membrance of me'" (1 Corinthians 11:23–24).
In a similar way, Jesus gave them a cup of wine
symbolizing His blood, "which is poured out
for many for the forgiveness of sins" (Matthew
26:28).

In other words, the Lord's Supper should always remind us of Jesus' death for us. He was
sinless and didn't deserve to die—but He will-
ingly took our sins upon Himself, and by His
death on the cross He purchased our salvation.
The Bible says, "The blood of Jesus, his Son,
purifies us from all sin" (1 John 1:7).

Don't ever let the Lord's Supper become something ordinary or boring. It tells us about the
greatest event in human history, Jesus' death for
us. May God use it to remind you of His love.[1]

There you have a summary of my answer to your
question, in the shortest and clearest way I can put it.

LEWIS: Thank you, Billy. It is indeed admirably clear
and simple.

GRAHAM: And I am very interested in hearing your
reaction to it. Because I think yours would be the
typical reaction of a member of your church. Is that
so?

LEWIS: I hope it is, yes. I am not a heretic, or even an
original theological thinker, but just a plain ordinary

---

[1] The quotation Graham reads comes verbatim from a September
24, 2007, online newsletter *Answers* from the Billy Graham Evangelistic Association. I altered only the date. But I think this is what
Graham would have said in Lewis' day as well as decades later.

layman of my branch of the Church, the Church of England. But if you don't mind my asking, what do you think I would say to it? What do you think we Anglicans believe about the Eucharist?

GRAHAM: Well, from what I understand from *Mere Christianity*, I am thinking—and also hoping—that you agree with everything I said in that statement, especially with my hope that the two of us are believing *essentially* the same thing, even if not *completely* the same thing; that whatever theological differences we have about it, and whatever you would want to add to what I said about it, these are not crucially important.

LEWIS: Why not?

GRAHAM: Because a sacrament is a sign, right?

LEWIS: Yes.

GRAHAM: And the whole point of a sign is to mean something, to point to something beyond itself, right?

LEWIS: Yes.

GRAHAM: And what this sign means is the fact that Christ died for our sins. And I think you agree with that. Do you?

LEWIS: I do, of course. But a sacrament is a supernatural sign, not just a natural, man-made sign. And that gives it the power actually to effect, or bring about, what it signifies. The water of Baptism, for example, signifies washing or cleansing, but it also does cleanse the soul. And it also signifies death by drowning, and it also really does make the soul die to the flesh and rise to the life in the Spirit, die to sin and rise to eternal life. And so we believe that the Eucharist does not only signify the Body and Blood of Christ given to us for our salvation but makes it really present.

So I don't deny anything in that statement you read, but I'd add something to it, something very important.

But let me begin with my agreements. May I have a copy of that so that I can respond to it point by point?

GRAHAM: Of course. Here.

LEWIS [he speed-reads it, makes a few quick marks, and then responds]: Well, I certainly agree that the churches differ about it, as you say in your first line. The question is how important those differences are. I also certainly agree that the differences between even the most extremely opposite beliefs about the Lord's Supper are almost nothing compared to the differences between a Christian and a non-Christian. It's clearly the same Christ that we both worship, even though I believe in what we call His Real Presence in the Eucharist and you, I think, do not, at least not in the way I do.

GRAHAM: So how do you see our difference?

LEWIS: I think you believe that the bread and wine are really only a holy symbol, and not the very substance or essence or reality of Christ's Body and Blood, isn't that right?

GRAHAM: Yes, but . . .

LEWIS: So you don't believe in the Real Presence.

GRAHAM: But I do! I believe He is really present to us when we receive the Lord's Supper with faith and love and devotion.

LEWIS: *How* is He present? Only in the same way He is present when a Christian reads the Bible or prays?

GRAHAM: No, I think it's more than that. He is present in a special way, an especially holy way, a way that He Himself ordained and commanded. That was His reason for ordaining this sacrament!

LEWIS [pressing]: Then where is our difference?

GRAHAM: I do not believe that He is present in the bread and wine or behind the appearance of the bread and wine in some miraculous change of substance or "transubstantiation", but I believe He is really and truly and personally present in our hearts and souls —which seems to me much more important than whether He is present in the bread and wine, in fact the essential thing. Because even if He *is* present in the bread and wine, or behind their appearances, His whole purpose in that is to become more present in our hearts and souls.

LEWIS: Of course that is the essential thing, and I think a Roman Catholic like Tollers here would agree about that, too, just as much as I would. [Tolkien nods, though apparently with some reservation.] We all agree on that "most essential thing". But I think we disagree about a second thing.

GRAHAM: But the second thing is only *second* in importance.

LEWIS: Only relative to the first thing, not in itself. In other words, second things are not reduced in importance just because there is some "first thing" above them that is even more important. The human body is tremendously important, and whether it lives or dies, and that's why whether someone is killing it, by murder or suicide, is extremely important. But the soul is even more important; and so whether it lives or dies eternally and whether sin is killing it is even more important. But that doesn't render the body less important than it would be without the importance of the soul. In fact, the importance of the soul makes that of the body much greater, because body and soul are so close and influence each other and ultimately share the same eternal destiny together.

So that's my principle about first and second things. Now, how do I apply that to the Sacrament? I believe that Christ makes Himself present in the Sacrament itself and not only in our souls. And I believe that whether He is present in our souls is much more important than whether He is present in the Sacrament, just as you said, and that the whole purpose of His making Himself present in the Sacrament is to make Himself more present in our souls. But that does not make it any less important whether He is present in the Sacrament. In fact, the fact that it is for our souls that He makes Himself bodily present in the Sacrament—that makes His bodily presence in the Sacrament *more* important, not less.

GRAHAM: I follow that reasoning. But our faith makes Him really present in our souls. What more do you think we need?

LEWIS: That's not the question. The question is: What more did *He* think we needed? What more did He give us?

GRAHAM: And you claim that He gave us more than faith alone could give us?

LEWIS: In one sense, no, because faith gives us Him, and nothing can be added to Him. But in another sense, yes, because we are bodies as well as souls, so He provided for both. The body can't have faith, but the body can have His Body.

GRAHAM: But only for the sake of strengthening our faith.

LEWIS: Yes.

GRAHAM: And it also presupposes faith—the faith that believes in and asks for Christ in the soul. You don't give the Sacrament to unbelievers.

LEWIS: That's right.

GRAHAM: Then the difference between us is not so terribly important.

LEWIS: I think it is. I believe that presence is objective, not just subjective; that His presence does not depend on our faith.

GRAHAM: So if His presence doesn't depend on our faith, why don't you give the Sacrament to unbelievers? If it's as objective as medicine, why not give it to the patient when he is comatose?

LEWIS: Because it's a gift, and a gift must be freely and consciously received as well as freely and consciously given.

GRAHAM: So does it or does it not depend on our faith how much grace we receive when we receive Communion?

LEWIS: It does.

GRAHAM: So it *does* depend on our faith. And faith is not objective, like rain falling from the sky, but subjective, like drinking the raindrops.

LEWIS: *How much* of His grace we get depends on our faith. That is indeed subjective. But whether it's His grace and His Real Presence and His divine life or not does not depend on our faith. That's objective. The amount of water that gets into our stomach depends on how much we open our mouths. But the water comes into us from the real clouds; it's not generated from us, like the sweat on our bodies.

GRAHAM: I understand. But that seems to be more a theological subtlety of theory than something that makes a great difference in practice.

LEWIS: I do not see it that way. It seems very important to me for practical reasons, not just theological reasons. Because the real, objective presence of Our Lord in the Sacrament invites us to stop putting our faith in our faith and simply put it in Him, in complete self-forgetfulness and adoration.

GRAHAM: I see. And I agree with your end—self-forgetful adoration—but not with your means—believing that Christ is present in the elements of the Sacrament.

LEWIS: That's not my main reason for believing it; that's just a practical payoff, so to speak. My main reason for believing it is that He has revealed it, He has told us, both in the Church and in the Bible.

GRAHAM: I believe the different things that I believe for the same reason: His authority, although I don't accept the Church as a divine authority like the Bible. So I think we disagree about our authorities. And we also differ on the means—does He get into our souls by faith or also by the matter of the Sacrament—but we agree on the end—His getting into our souls and lives. As you say, the second things are important. But the first thing is more important.

LEWIS: Yes, but I think I disagree about *how* important our disagreement about that second thing is.

And here is another difference between us, I think, about both the means and the end, both the Sacrament and the soul. I see His presence in us as including our bodies as well as our souls and as including His Body as well as His soul. I believe that since He made us with bodies as well as souls, He wants to make Himself present also in our bodies and present by His Body.

GRAHAM: But you agree that He is most of all concerned with our souls, don't you?

LEWIS: Of course.

GRAHAM: So I think we agree on three things: that we have a real agreement, that we have a real disagreement, and that what we agree about is much more important than what we disagree about.

LEWIS: I agree with all three of those points. And yet the disagreement remains, and remains just as important in itself as it was before we added the agreement about the first thing, or the "big picture". In fact, more so, since it's not separable from that first thing, or that "big picture". To put it concretely, our disagreement is important because it's about Christ, not just about sacramental theology.

GRAHAM: Do you also agree with the three reasons I gave for celebrating the Lord's Supper in that statement from my organization?

LEWIS: Let's see. The first is that, as you say, "this has been true since the beginning of the Christian faith." We Anglicans, like the Roman Catholics, call that "Sacred Tradition", not just human, man-made tradition—at least those who call ourselves "Anglo-Catholics".

The second is that, as you say, "Jesus told His disciples to do it until He comes again." It's a commandment, not an option.

And the third is that the Bible clearly teaches it.

So I agree with all that, of course . . .

GRAHAM: So we are really pretty much on the same page here.

LEWIS: But not wholly. [He reads Graham's statement.] You next say that "Jesus gave them a cup of wine *symbolizing* His blood." We believe it's not just a symbol; it really is His blood. [Graham frowns.]

I have another disagreement with your statement, I think. You say, "the Lord's Supper should always *remind* us of Jesus' death for us." Of course that's true, but we believe it's not just a reminder, like a mental picture. It's not like gazing at a stained glass window or an icon. He's really there. That is really Christ, even though it doesn't look like Him. (In fact, it looks much less like Him than a stained glass window or an icon does.)

5

Lewis' Faith and Graham's Critique

GRAHAM: Well, I understand that you believe that, but I don't. I know that's in your tradition, but that's an extra-biblical tradition.

LEWIS: No, I don't think that's true. It comes from the Bible. He didn't say, "This *symbolizes* My Body" and "This *symbolizes* My blood"; He said, "This *is* My Body" and "This *is* My Blood." It's not extra-biblical, it's biblical. I think it's *your* position that is extra-biblical. It's you who add to His words. You add the word "symbolizes".

GRAHAM: Well, we both believe all the words in the Bible, but we just interpret them differently.

LEWIS: I don't see how you can dismiss the question of interpretation so easily.

GRAHAM: I don't dismiss it. It's a crucial question.

LEWIS: Sorry. I accept your correction. But you do dismiss something else much too easily, I think.

GRAHAM: What?

LEWIS: The historical fact that all Christians in the world, except for a few heretics, interpreted those words in my way, literally, not in your way, symbolically, for 1500 years until the Reformation.

GRAHAM: Well, even if that's so (and I think it's a bit of an exaggeration or an oversimplification), I believe that interpretation is still only a human tradition, not the Bible itself. That's added to the Bible. So it can be wrong.

LEWIS: No, we don't think so. We think our interpretation of His words, as well as the words themselves, are right there in the Bible.

GRAHAM: Where?

LEWIS: In the very next words He says there in Matthew: "which is poured out for many *for the forgiveness of sins*". A mere symbol does not have the power to forgive sins! That's why the blood of bulls and goats in Old Testament Judaism couldn't forgive sins, as the Bible explains in the Epistle to the Hebrews: because their blood was only a symbol of His blood. The sacrificial lambs in Judaism were only symbols; they were not "the lamb of God who takes away the sins of the world".

GRAHAM: We believe He takes away the sins of the world by shedding His blood on the Cross, not by instituting the sacrament.

LEWIS: But in this passage, Matthew is describing the Lord's Supper here, not just the Cross. That's the context.

GRAHAM: I understand what you believe and why you believe it, and I respect your motives and your argument, but you haven't proved to me that your interpretation is the right one.

LEWIS: I wasn't trying to prove it to you. You didn't ask me to do that. You asked me to explain what I believed and why I believed it.

GRAHAM: Fair enough. But I still think our disagreement is secondary, because what we both *do*, when we celebrate this sacrament, we both do out of our common faith in and love for Him, to obey His command, and that is more important than how we understand it and interpret it differently. As you yourself wrote somewhere, "He said, take and eat; he did not say take and understand."

LEWIS: I am hoisted on my own petard! That's true. In fact, we *don't* understand it. At least not adequately. Nobody does. It's a great mystery. It's a miracle.

GRAHAM: Could we say, then, that our theologies are different, but our religion is the same?

LEWIS: Yes, if you mean by that that the *object* of our religion is the same Christ and also that the *motive* behind believing the different things we believe is the same: we put our faith in Him, and we want to be faithful to Him, to obey what we believe is His will. That's why Tollers is a Roman Catholic and believes in the Real Presence and all the other things his church teaches; and that's why you're a Protestant Evangelical, and you don't believe all the things he does; and that's why as an Anglican I don't fully agree with either of you. What we believe isn't the same, but *why* we believe it is. Our Lord is the same, and our motive is the same: fidelity to Him.

GRAHAM: Good! We do indeed agree about where we agree and where we disagree. But I still wonder how important our disagreements are about the Lord's Supper. I think what's infinitely more important is what we *don't* disagree about, namely, faith. That's what saves us, not the Lord's Supper.

LEWIS: Well, now, I don't want to be contentious, but that's precisely one of the most important things that *does* divide us.

GRAHAM: What? Do you believe there are two ways to be saved, faith or the sacraments?

LEWIS: No. That's not an "either/or". It's a "both/and".

GRAHAM: Can the sacraments save us without faith?

LEWIS: No.

GRAHAM: And can faith save us without the sacraments?

LEWIS: Yes. God can work outside His sacraments. But He also works by His sacraments.

GRAHAM: So the sacraments can actually save you?

LEWIS: Yes.

GRAHAM: Well, I don't believe that.

LEWIS: Why not?

GRAHAM: Because the Bible doesn't say that. Why do you believe it?

LEWIS: Because the Bible does say that.

GRAHAM: Well, now we're talking about two different interpretations again.

LEWIS: No, we're not. We're talking about a very clear and direct statement. First Peter 3:21 says, "Baptism saves you." There it is, word for word.

GRAHAM: Only because Baptism is the symbol and expression of saving faith, but it's our faith that saves us.

LEWIS: But that's not the Bible itself. It's your interpretation of it.

GRAHAM: I suppose so.

LEWIS: But don't you say we don't need anyone or anything else outside the Bible to interpret the Bible, like a church, or Tradition? Don't you say the Bible interprets itself?

GRAHAM: Yes, and that is exactly what I am doing. I am interpreting this text in the Bible by what the rest of the Bible says.

LEWIS: Where does it say in any other verse in the Bible that He is *not* really present in His sacraments and that they do *not* have the power to communicate His salvation and His divine life to us?

GRAHAM: "God is a Spirit, and they that worship Him must worship Him in spirit and in truth."

LEWIS: That's the text the Gnostic heretics used to deny the Incarnation! God is a Spirit, indeed, but He took to Himself a human body and soul in the Incarnation, and He continues to work through material instruments: us. We worship "in spirit" but also in the body, because we *are* in bodies. We don't have an out-of-the-body experience when we worship.

GRAHAM: Don't you think my interpretation is reasonable?

LEWIS: Of course it is. Every heresy in history sounded reasonable. And God's way of doing things sounded unreasonable. God always surprises us.

GRAHAM: That is true. But that doesn't prove that "Baptism saves you" is not what I say: a kind of shorthand for "the faith that Baptism expresses saves you."

LEWIS: No it doesn't. So I agree that I haven't proved my point to you.

GRAHAM: And you must admit that mine is a reasonable and a possible interpretation.

LEWIS: Well, yes, though as a literary critic, I find it rather strained and sophisticated and not the one ordinary readers would take. And the Bible is written for ordinary people, not sophisticated scholars and theologians.

GRAHAM: Is that your main argument?

LEWIS: No, my main argument is that your interpretation is not the one the whole mass of Christians made for 1500 years.

GRAHAM: In other words, it's not the way your church and its tradition interprets it.

LEWIS: It's not the way *anyone* interpreted it until the Reformation.

GRAHAM: I think you are oversimplifying Church history a bit there. But I'm not a historian or a scholar, so I can't argue with you about the details, but my principle is simple and clear: I don't accept any church or any tradition as infallible. So even if that's what your church taught for 1500 years, that doesn't make it infallibly right.

LEWIS: It was your church, too, until Luther split it. There was only one, remember?

GUY: Jack, don't you think you are turning this friendly dialogue among Christians into an Oxford debate?

GRAHAM: No, let him argue like an Oxford debater. I don't mind. My point is simple. I believe the only infallible authority is the Bible itself. I believe in *sola scriptura*. And that's also why I believe in *sola fide*, too: because the Bible says that we're saved by faith, not by faith plus any good works of ours, including the work of being baptized or receiving Holy Communion.

LEWIS: But here again it's the Bible that seems very clearly to contradict you. It says, very clearly, that we are *not* saved by faith alone. It's there, word for word, in James 2:24: "So you see that a man is justified by works and not by faith alone." How much clearer and more explicit could it possibly be?

GUY: I've been keeping quiet for a long time here, guys, but I just have to put in my two cents' worth now. Jack, you said at the beginning that you had deep respect for Billy, here, but I think you've been pretty harsh with him for the last few minutes—treating him as if he didn't know his Bible or as if he were a heretic.

LEWIS: Goodness, gracious, I never meant to do that! Perhaps I just got so lost in the argument that I forgot that other people have feelings as well as intellects. People tell me I do that habitually. I apologize —not for what I said but for how I said it. I meant no offense.

GRAHAM: And I took no offense, Jack. So let's get back to the point. Here's an argument for you: If it's not faith alone but also good works that save us, if we can't be saved without good works added to our faith, then the Good Thief was not saved, because he had no time for good works, only faith alone. But Jesus told him, "Today you will be with me in Paradise." And Jesus certainly made no mistakes.

LEWIS: That's a good argument. And it proves that God *can* save you, or justify you, without good works, at least in exceptional cases like his. But the Good Thief's circumstances were exceptional, weren't they? Aren't there also hundreds of other passages in the Bible, addressed to all of us, in ordinary circumstances, that say that we will be judged by our works?

GRAHAM: Yes, but only if they are the works of love that come from faith.

LEWIS: But love for a Christian is not a feeling. Love for a Christian means the *works* of love.

GRAHAM: It's true that love is proved by its works. But it's also true that our love, as Christians, is rooted in our faith.

LEWIS: That's also true. But . . .

TOLKIEN [interrupting]: I thought you two were supposed to be arguing about the sacraments, not about justification or salvation. That's another issue, isn't it?

LEWIS: Yes, but the two issues are parallel. In both, the Bible teaches (or very strongly seems to teach) the opposite of "faith alone".

TOLKIEN: What is the relation of that to the sacraments?

LEWIS: That even though God *can* save you by faith alone without the sacraments of Baptism and Holy Communion in some cases, yet He instituted the sacraments as normal ways by which He saves you and puts His own eternal life into you.

GRAHAM: But both the sacraments and good works don't "take", so to speak, don't count, don't save you, without faith.

LEWIS: True. But faith doesn't work without them, either.

GRAHAM: It did with the Good Thief.

LEWIS: Yes, but it doesn't do that usually.

GRAHAM: So you say that God saves us by faith *and* the sacraments.

LEWIS: Yes: the sacraments that you receive because of your faith. You separate them—faith and sacraments—while I join them.

GRAHAM: Why?

LEWIS: Because I believe that Christ joined them.

GRAHAM: So the relation between faith and sacraments is the same as the relation between faith and works.

LEWIS: Yes. And just as He usually saves you by faith *and* the good works that you do because of your faith, He usually saves you by faith *and* the sacraments you receive by faith. It's a both/and, not an either/or in both cases.

GRAHAM: I agree that the Bible teaches that both good works and the sacraments of Baptism and Holy Communion are commanded. They are the natural expression of our faith. But when we do good works, including the work of receiving the sacraments, it's the faith element that saves us, not the work element.

LEWIS: The Bible doesn't say that.

GRAHAM: Yes it does. The Apostle Paul says in his letter to the Romans that Abraham was justified by faith alone without the works of the law.

LEWIS: Paul didn't say that. Luther put the word "alone" in there. It's not in the original Greek.

GRAHAM: But it still reads: "So you see then that a man is justified by faith without the works of the law."

LEWIS: I think Paul is speaking there about the liturgical law, the Jewish liturgical sacrifices there, not the works of love.

GRAHAM: No, I think he's talking about the Ten Commandments, which Christ summarized as love—to love God with our whole hearts and our neighbors as ourselves.

LEWIS: In any case, in other passages Paul seems to say we are not saved without good works. And Our Lord clearly says the same thing in the parable of the last judgment. We will be judged by our works, by the works of love.

GRAHAM: Only if they are the works of faith. We're not saved without faith.

LEWIS: That's true. But when we receive the sacraments in faith or do the works of love because of our faith, why do you think it's only the faith element and not the sacrament element or the charity element that saves us? Saint Paul ranks charity even above faith in 1 Corinthians 13.

GRAHAM: Because faith is spiritual, not physical, but the sacraments and the works of love are physical. The physical is important only because it's an expression of the spiritual.

LEWIS: So you assume that only the element that is spiritual can save us.

GRAHAM: Of course. Don't you?

LEWIS: No. I think we are saved by something physical. Buddha and Socrates and all the great philosophers claimed to save us by saying, "This is my
mind", but Christ saved us by saying, "This is My
Body"—on the Cross and in the Sacrament. We're
saved by Christ's death on the Cross, and that death
was a physical death, not a spiritual death; so we
are saved by something physical. You yourself believe
that, I think.

GRAHAM: I believe that His physical death saves us,
yes. I understand that, but I don't understand how He
saves us by a little water being poured on our head,
or by eating bread and drinking wine. That sounds
to me too much like magic or a fairy tale.

LEWIS: I don't think any of us really understand just
how any of those things work, including how His
physical death on the Cross saves us. There were half
a dozen theories of the Atonement, and the Church
never dogmatically endorsed any one of them as the
definitive explanation, except to deny Luther's theory
that it was only a legal fiction and not a real transformation. Luther called us, even after we accepted
Christ, only "a pile of dung covered by snow".

I don't understand just how the sacraments work,
either. But that doesn't mean that they don't work. I
don't understand much of how the physical universe
works, either—science is always discovering more
things, and more incredible things, about the universe—but it does work, whether I understand it or
not. You say you can't understand how He saves us
by having a little water poured on us or by having
what looks like ordinary bread and wine taken into

us. Neither can I! But the fact that I can't understand it doesn't mean it's not true.

GRAHAM: But how can matter act on spirit?

LEWIS: I don't know how, but I know—we both know —that in fact it does. Someone hits you, and that makes you angry. Someone hugs you, and that makes you happy.

GRAHAM: That's true.

LEWIS: Because God made us with bodies as well as souls, together, so He deals with us as bodies and souls together, not as souls alone or as souls and bodies separately. That was the heresy of the Gnostics: they were purely spiritual. *Terribly* "spiritual". Chesterton says that the Incarnation saved us from that, from "spirituality—a dreadful doom". A lot of people today who would never darken the door of any church say they are "spiritual" instead of religious. What that always means is Gnosticism: immateriality instead of anything material.

GRAHAM: I agree that religion is more than spirituality.

LEWIS: The word "religion" literally means "relationship", "binding relationship", or "a relationship that binds us back to our Creator". And what gets related to God is not an angel but a human being. And a human being is a whole, with a body as well as a soul.

GRAHAM: I don't disagree with that.

LEWIS: Well, that's why religion—a relationship between God and man—includes both faith and sacraments and both faith and works. That's why God instituted sacraments. Angels can't use them. Angels don't need them. We do.

GRAHAM: I agree with that all that in principle, but not with the sacramental theology that you deduce from it. But perhaps I'm misunderstanding your theology. Can you tell me exactly what you do believe about Holy Communion?

LEWIS: I put it as simply and clearly as I could in *Mere Christianity*. And here is Tollers' copy. Let me try to find the passage. [He turns a few pages of the book to find it.] Here it is: "There are three things that spread the Christ-life to us. . . ."

GRAHAM: You mean by "the Christ-life" salvation, right?

LEWIS: Yes, salvation, sanctifying grace, justification, being born again, regeneration, eternal life, *zoe*, supernatural life, becoming a child of God, adoption, atonement, reconciliation—they're all different names for essentially the same thing or aspects of the same thing, aren't they?

GRAHAM: Essentially, yes, though different Christians explain it differently or emphasize different aspects of it and call it by different names.

LEWIS: And the three things that do it are: "baptism, belief, and that mysterious action which different Christians call by different names—Holy Communion, the Mass, the Lord's Supper".

GRAHAM: And I say it all comes down to only *one* thing on our part, that it's *sola fide*, that it's faith alone that actually saves us. God alone saves us, of course, and His grace alone saves us, but it's our faith that accepts it. And that's enough. I just can't understand how sacraments can do it, how a material action of water or bread or wine can cause a spiritual effect.

LEWIS: And as I said a minute ago, neither can I! That's the next thing I said in the book: "I cannot myself see why these things should be the conductors of the new kind of life. But then, if one did not happen to know, I should never have seen any connection between a particular physical pleasure and the appearance of a new human being in the world." In other words, the connection between sex and the beginning of natural life. "We have to take reality as it comes to us; there is no good jabbering about what it ought to be like or what we should have expected it to be like. But though I cannot see why it should be so, I can tell you why I believe it is so . . . Jesus was (and is) God. And it seems plain as a matter of history that He taught His followers that the new life was communicated in this way. In other words, I believe it on His authority."

GRAHAM: I think my first principle, my reason for believing what I believe, is the same as yours: the authority of Christ.

LEWIS: But Christ taught these things about Baptism and Communion.

GRAHAM: I don't believe He did.

LEWIS: The Bible says He did. And all the Christians in the world until the Protestant Reformation believed that He did.

GRAHAM: I think they got their interpretation of the Bible wrong. That's why I'm not a Catholic, not even an Anglo-Catholic.

LEWIS: But the reason you gave for preferring your interpretation to theirs, the reason for not believing these Catholic things, was that you just couldn't understand how or why God would act on our spirits through matter. But "I can't understand that" doesn't entail the conclusion that "that can't be true" because if it did, we'd have to reject most of the mysteries of the Christian faith, including the Incarnation itself.

GRAHAM: Oh, I agree with your principle there again. And I don't deny the material aspect of human nature or of religion or the importance of the sacraments. I simply say faith comes first, not sacraments. You yourself admitted that sacraments can't save you without faith but faith can save you without sacraments. The sacraments are relative to faith, expressions of faith or means to faith, not ends.

LEWIS: I think I agree with that, too.

GRAHAM: So where do we differ?

LEWIS: I think the difference between us is that I see the relation between faith and sacraments as a both/and, not an either/or.

GRAHAM: But I don't deny the sacraments. I just say that the two parts of your both/and (faith and sacraments) are not equal. Faith without sacraments is something that can save you. You agreed with that, right? The Good Thief, remember?

LEWIS: Yes.

GRAHAM: And sacraments without faith cannot save you. You believe that, don't you? They're not impersonal magic.

LEWIS: Right.

GRAHAM: And didn't you agree that sacraments are relative to faith, to express and to strengthen our faith?

LEWIS: I agree that one of their ends is to strengthen our faith, yes. But that does not necessarily mean they are relative to our faith. I do not agree that Christ is present in the sacraments only if we have faith. I believe He is really present, objectively present, independent of us.

GRAHAM: Because that's what your Church teaches.

LEWIS: Yes, but also for other reasons.

GRAHAM: Give me one.

LEWIS: All right. The object of faith has to be something real, right? That real object has to exist before faith in it can exist. Christ has to exist before we can have faith in Him.

GRAHAM: Of course.

LEWIS: And the same thing must be true of His presence in the Sacrament: our faith can't cause the Real Presence. We can't have faith in it if it's not really there.

GRAHAM: So what does that prove?

LEWIS: That our faith is relative to and dependent on His presence, and therefore His presence cannot be relative to and dependent on our faith.

GRAHAM: So you don't think that the sacraments are relative to our faith? I thought you said the opposite a moment ago.

LEWIS: I have to make a philosophical distinction here. They are not relative to our faith in the order of efficient causality. Faith is not the *efficient* cause of the sacraments. It's not their origin; faith doesn't make them or make them work. God does that. But I think the strengthening of our faith is the *final* cause of the sacraments, the end or purpose of the sacraments. I believe that God instituted the sacraments as means to test our faith and to elicit our faith and to strengthen our faith.

GRAHAM: Well, I think that makes sense. And why do you think the sacraments do that? Why do they strengthen our faith?

LEWIS: Faith always has to go beyond three things: it has to go beyond appearances to our senses, beyond our rational understanding, and beyond our feelings. And the sacraments do all three things. Especially the Eucharist. In Baptism, the appearance of the water, which we use to wash away visible, physical dirt, at least suggests invisible, spiritual cleansing from sin; but in the Eucharist, the appearances don't even suggest what it really is. Christ's Body doesn't look like a piece of bread. Tomorrow morning a priest will give me a little round, thin, cold, tasteless wafer that looks like bread. And it is not what it looks like.

Nor is it what reason alone can know: I can't prove that it isn't merely bread by reason alone.

And when I receive it, I will not have a "religious experience". I will believe in His presence, and I will love His presence, but I will not feel His presence. The feeling is a gift, and He only occasionally gives it.

So it's not my senses or my imagination; and it's not my reason or my understanding; and it's not my feelings or my experience; but it's only my faith that tells me that that is not what it seems to be, that this is Christ Himself hiding behind what seems to be only bread and wine.

GRAHAM: Jack, even though I don't believe exactly what you believe, I respect your faith and I admire much of what you say. I certainly do not reject the sacraments. I accept them and I love them because Christ instituted them. The Bible tells me that. They are holy! And I believe He really acts on me through them, as He does through His Word the Bible and through prayer. He's really there *doing things to us*. In that sense, I believe in His "real presence" there, too. I just don't think of it in the same way as you do. You think that somehow the very matter acts on our spirit. When I think about that, I simply can't understand *how* matter can act on spirit. Yet as you say, it does when we are slapped or when we are hugged. I'm afraid I'm just not a philosopher.

LEWIS: Oh, I think even the philosophers have great difficulty understanding profound things like hugs and slaps. They're much better at understanding abstractions.

GRAHAM [laughing]: I know what you mean. I'm with you there. My bottom line is just this: The sacraments are an important part of my Christian faith, just as they are for you. But they are not what I rely on; Christ is. They do not save me; Christ does. I do not look at them when I receive them; I look at Christ. They are totally transparent to Christ.

LEWIS: I agree that it's good that you look along them instead of at them—that's what He meant us to do. I agree that the sacraments are not what we ultimately have faith in: Christ is. Of course it's only Christ that saves us; His sacraments, like our faith, are only the means He uses. But He does really use these means, so in a secondary sense, they are rightful objects of our faith when we "look along" them to Him. (Although even in that secondary sense, it's not good to have faith in our own faith, but it *is* good to have faith in His sacraments.)

GRAHAM: I'm just concerned that we put all our faith in the Person of Christ, not in the impersonal means He uses.

LEWIS: But what if He puts Himself into the things He uses? What if He makes Himself really present in the sacraments?

GRAHAM: You believe He does that, but I do not. So I do not see how it's right to put our faith in the sacraments. I'm not sure about this "looking along" stuff, this "secondary" aspect of faith.

LEWIS: Do you believe the Bible?

GRAHAM: Yes.

LEWIS: Do you trust it to do its job and tell us only the truth, and the most important truth that there is?

GRAHAM: Yes.

LEWIS: Is that because you believe it is the Word of God?

GRAHAM: Yes. If it were only a human book, I would not trust it so completely.

LEWIS: Well, there you are. I believe He uses the sacraments at least as much as He uses the Bible. I look-along both, I don't just look at them.

GRAHAM: But you worship the Sacrament of the Lord's Supper. You look at it as well as looking along it.

LEWIS: Only because I believe He is really present in it. That's why it actually "effects what it signifies". That's the traditional Catholic definition of a sacrament. The Bible is holy and authoritative, but it is not a sacrament. I worship the God of the Bible, but I don't worship the Bible, because it's not Him, it's just His Word. So when I have faith in the Bible, I'm doing it only because I'm looking along it at Him. He's the ultimate object of my faith, and the Bible is a secondary or reflective or proximate object of my faith because it's His word. You still look confused. I've been too abstract. Here, look at a secular example of the principle. Suppose you are in a battle, and you are about to be slain with a sword, and King Arthur appears to save you, wielding Excalibur. Your faith is in Arthur primarily, but it is also in his sword secondarily.

GRAHAM: That's a good example, because the Bible itself uses it: it calls itself "the sword of the Spirit, which is the Word of God", and it says that this sword "pierces the heart and distinguishes the soul and the spirit as a butcher's knife distinguishes the bone and the sinews".

GUY: So where, exactly, do you two agree, and where do you disagree?

LEWIS: Let's see whether I can sort out our agreements and disagreements. We both believe He instituted the sacraments—two, at least—and commanded us to celebrate them. We both believe they are holy because of that and also because He acts on us through them, whether materially or spiritually. And we both believe we should put our faith ultimately in Him alone but also, secondarily, in the means He uses, including the sacraments and the Bible.

But I adore the Sacrament, or direct my adoration to Him in the Sacrament, as you do not, because I believe He is personally present in the Eucharist as He is not in the Bible.

GRAHAM: But the Bible is more important than the sacraments because it is God's infallible truth about everything, including the sacraments.

You say in *Mere Christianity* that God uses *three* means to save us, or to give us His eternal life—faith and Baptism and the Eucharist—and I think you'd expand that to four if you add the works of Christian love—but I say we are saved by faith alone; that just as good works are only the expressions of our faith in Christ, so the sacraments are also only expressions of our faith and symbols of our faith that Christ instituted. Do you think that is the essential place where we differ?

LEWIS: No, I don't think so. It's more concrete than that. Like Luther and like Roman Catholics, I believe that that thing which looks like a wafer of bread really is the Body of Christ, literally, not just symbolically. As literally as my tongue is literally here and moving in my mouth. And that is why I will kneel and adore It. You don't, because you don't believe that.

GRAHAM: But we both don't just look *at* the sacrament; rather, we look *along* the sacrament, as you say, and see Christ, with the eye of faith. For both of us, it is transparent to Christ.

LEWIS: But if that wafer is really not bread anymore but is Christ's own Body, then you can't say it is "transparent to Christ" because it *is* Christ. *Christ* cannot be "transparent to Christ"!

GRAHAM: But can't we say that the material appearances are transparent to Christ? We both believe they symbolize Christ—that's how they are transparent to Christ—but you also believe that they are the Body and Blood of Christ, that they are the thing they symbolize.

LEWIS: I don't think that will quite work, either, because the appearances are not at all transparent to Christ, as a holy picture would be. Bread does not look like Christ.

GRAHAM: True, it doesn't. So what do you say the appearances do if they do not merely symbolize Christ and if they are not Christ and if they are not "transparent to Christ"?

LEWIS: They hide Him. And that is the opposite of being "transparent to Christ". In fact, *nothing* here is "transparent to Christ". The accidents are not "transparent to Christ" because they do not look like Christ, and the substance is not "transparent to Christ" because it *is* Christ. So neither the substance nor the accidents, neither the essence nor the appearances, are "transparent to Christ".

GRAHAM: What about the Bible? Is that "transparent to Christ?"

LEWIS: Yes. It's like a holy picture made of words, symbols. That's why we believe the Blessed Sacrament is holier than the Bible. The Bible is only symbols of Christ, not Christ. The Eucharist *is* Christ, the very substance of Christ.

GRAHAM: What, exactly, does that mean? What do you mean by "substance"?

LEWIS: Aha, you have caught me on my weak point. I must confess I have great difficulty imagining or clearly conceiving what in the world the word "substance" means there. So I am not feeling very confident now in arguing about something I don't claim to understand.

So if you don't mind, I'd like to try to understand something that I suspect is much simpler and clearer, namely, what *you* believe about the Eucharist.

GRAHAM: What do you think I believe?

LEWIS: Well, first of all, you emphasize faith. When I sent the manuscript of *Mere Christianity* to five Christian friends of different denominations, two of the Protestants said they thought that topic was the only one I didn't emphasize enough: the primacy of faith. I think you would probably agree with that criticism, right?

GRAHAM: Yes, but I don't think it's a sharp disagreement; I think it's more a difference in emphasis.

LEWIS: I agree.

TOLKIEN: But you and I believe in the Real Presence, Jack, and Protestants do not.

LEWIS: Yes, that's true. But even there, I don't separate that from faith. I think I made the mistake, in *Mere Christianity*, of saying that the life of Christ in our souls is transmitted to us in three ways: by our act of faith, by Baptism, and by the Eucharist. That sounds as if I thought the three ways were not only different but independent of each other. I think that was a mistake because all three are matters of faith, including the Eucharist—though not of course "faith alone".

TOLKIEN: Wait a moment, please! What do you mean when you say that the Eucharist is a matter of faith? It sounds to me as if you're saying that His presence there depends on our faith.

LEWIS: No, I'm not saying that at all. I say the opposite, as you do: that Our Lord is really present there whether we believe it or not. But I think our faith is the purpose and end of the Eucharist.

TOLKIEN: One of them, at least. Who knows how many different ends or purposes God has in mind when He makes something as mysterious as the Eucharist?

LEWIS: Touché, Tollers.

TOLKIEN: So our faith is not, for you, in any sense the efficient cause in the Eucharist, but only a final cause, a purpose, right?

LEWIS: Right, I think. No . . . wait. In a way, in another way, it is an efficient cause.

TOLKIEN: How?

LEWIS: In this way: the reason we believe He is really present is because He said so, and we simply believe what He said. So in that sense, faith, not reason or sensation or feeling, is the cause—not of His presence, but of our adoration of the Eucharist.

TOLKIEN: That seems right.

GUY: But you believe it only because your church teaches it. So your faith is in your church.

TOLKIEN: It's not *my* church, it's God's Church. If it were mine, I'd never believe it.

LEWIS: The point, Guy, is that we don't believe in the Church as an *alternative* to believing in Christ or an addition to believing in Christ. We believe the Church only because Christ gave us the Church, and we believe in the Eucharist and in the Real Presence because it's what the Church—His Church—has always believed and taught.

GUY: You believe what you believe because your church teaches it. I believe what I believe because the Bible teaches it.

LEWIS: So we're back to that issue again.

TOLKIEN: But it's the Church that gave us the Bible. And that's how the whole Church has interpreted the Bible she gave us, for 1500 years. Was the Holy Spirit asleep all that time?

LEWIS: Tollers, I think that question—the question of the relation between the Church and the Bible—is not the question we should be debating now.

GUY: Why?

LEWIS: Because it's a diversion. We should stay focused on our topic, the Eucharist.

GRAHAM: I appreciate your logical focus, and I agree with you. Let's talk about the relation between the Bible and the Church later.

TOLKIEN: Fair enough.

GRAHAM: I was very encouraged by what you said about the whole point and purpose of the Eucharist being faith. Could you explain that a little more?

TOLKIEN: I'd like to hear that, too, for the opposite reason: I felt a little suspicious of it.

LEWIS: I shall try. I believe Our Lord hides in the Eucharist precisely to stimulate our faith. Let's analyze the concept of "hiding" for a moment. It seems to me it has two essential parts: real objective presence—the person who hides—and apparent absence to the observer. If He were not really there, He could not be hiding there. And if we saw Him, He would not be hiding there, either. And when I say, "saw Him", I mean three things: with our senses, with our reason, or with our feelings. If we saw Him there with our senses, if we proved He was there with our reason, or if we felt Him there with our emotions, our intuition, our interior senses, or however that works, then we wouldn't need faith at all, only sight or reason or feeling.

That's why Thomas Aquinas wrote in his Eucharistic hymn, "Sight, touch, and taste in Thee are each deceived; / The ear alone most safely is believed. / I believe all the Son of God has spoken; / Than Truth's own word there is no truer token."

GRAHAM: And can you tell me just what you mean by faith there?

LEWIS: I heard a skeptic quote a Fundamentalist pastor defining faith this way: "Here's what I mean by faith: God said it, I believe it, that settles it." That was supposed to be satirical, but I thought it was quite right, even though I'm not a Fundamentalist.

GRAHAM: Good! Even though I disagree with your theology, I admire your definition of faith. And also your motive for faith: not because I've proved it or because I feel it, but because God said it.

LEWIS: What, exactly, is your objection to my theology?

GUY: Aren't we supposed to be examining *Billy's* theology now?

LEWIS: Yes, we are, but I think it will come clearer this way, by contrasting it to mine.

GRAHAM: I can't help seeing yours as kind of materialistic.

LEWIS: That's what I thought you'd say. So let's explore that objection.

GRAHAM: Good. You said you thought the end or point of the Eucharist was faith, didn't you?

LEWIS: Yes.

GRAHAM: And faith is a spiritual act, isn't it? An act of our soul, first of all, even if it's expressed in a bodily way?

LEWIS: Yes, it is.

GRAHAM: Well, that's why I center on the spiritual aspect of the Eucharist, Christ's spiritual presence in our souls, rather than the material aspect, whether He's present in the bread and the wine.

TOLKIEN: He is not present in the bread and wine because it isn't bread and wine anymore.

LEWIS: Well, that's the whole bone of contention, isn't it? Whether that's just physical matter, as it appears to be, or the Second Person of the divine Trinity hiding behind those appearances.

GRAHAM: Yes, I suppose that is where we clearly contradict each other.

LEWIS: And that's certainly much more than just a difference in emphasis or perspective or approach, or anything like that.

GRAHAM: I guess it is. I don't believe that the bread and wine literally turn into the Body and Blood of Christ "out there". I believe the transformation takes place in here, in us, in our souls, by God's grace and by our faith to receive it. And both of those things are spiritual, even if they're expressed by those physical things, by the bread and the wine. And I don't think that makes me a spiritualist or an immaterialist or a Gnostic heretic any more than I think that your faith that He is present in a more material way makes you a materialist. So I think our difference *is* more of a difference in emphasis than a sharp line drawn in the sand.

LEWIS: Hmmm—perhaps.

GRAHAM: I have a sense, deep down, that our two positions are much closer together than they seem, closer than most people think they are. Yet I also sense that there is also a real line drawn in the sand, as you say. I can't help thinking you are worshipping a holy picture, and that is a kind of idolatry, even if you have the best and holiest of intentions. So I sense that we are both very close to each other *and* very far.

LEWIS: I sense the same two things—our closeness and our farness—and I think God has called both of us not to add fuel to the fire of division by arguing about our differences in public, but to fight on that part of the battlefield which I called "mere Christianity", where the ranks are the thinnest and the issues are the thickest, the largest, and the most momentous.

GUY: If I may make a suggestion here, can we get back to Billy's objection to Lewis' theology instead of arguing about how far apart your two theologies are?

LEWIS: I think that's a very good idea, Guy.

GUY: Jack, you have had plenty of time to criticize Billy by now, but he was too polite to criticize you at any length. I think justice demands equal time and attention to his objections, don't you?

LEWIS: I do indeed. So let's explore them now, shall we? Are you on board with that agenda, Billy?

GRAHAM: All right. But let me just take a breath and a bit of tea before we do that.

Christopher, who was waiting silently in the wings, brings in a hot pot of tea and fresh crumpets. He has to remind the four of them that the food and tea is there. They still are too busy thinking and talking to eat. Graham, seeing this, asks:

GRAHAM: I know you two love to talk over a pint of Guinness. So I know you can talk and drink at the same time. But you haven't touched your tea. If you want to drink something stronger while we talk, please don't let me be an obstacle. I do not think of you as alcoholics, even secretly. I know the Apostle Paul recommended wine to Timothy—"drink a little

wine for your stomach's sake"—so I'm not a teeto-
taler on principle, just in practice. And I'm not op-
posed to anyone ever smoking, in principle, and I'm
not allergic to smoke, even though I don't smoke myself; so please feel free to light up if you want. I suspect you're both being over-polite for my sake.

LEWIS: Oh, no, we're not as polite as you think we
are. Our ancestors, now—they were much more polite and proper and formal than we are, and they
were probably right. I think we British are becoming
more and more American every day. Oh, I'm sorry, I
didn't mean that as an insult to you; I almost forgot
you were an American.

TOLKIEN: But you did mean it as an insult to Americans.

LEWIS [smiling ruefully]: Ah, we all have our little
secret sins and prejudices, I suppose—until a wiz-
ard like Gandalf here exposes them. But seriously,
Billy, the only reason we were not smoking or drinking is because we were so interested in our conversation that we simply forgot there was anything else in
the world. Including our wonderful servant Christopher here. [Turns around and turns everyone's attention to Christopher.] Thanks, Christopher, for doing
Martha's work so very well while the four of us are
all stumbling and bumbling in trying to do Mary's
work, but not as successfully. [Reflectively, tentatively,
to no one in particular:] I think it's much easier to
feel you've succeeded in the active life than in the
contemplative life, don't you? Especially if the people actually eat and drink what you serve them instead

of being too absentminded to notice it! But no matter how many *words* we eat, we're never satisfied that
we're quite finished with that food until our bodies tell us we're finished and we get sleepy. I don't
think minds ever get sleepy, only the bodies they're
attached to.

TOLKIEN: That's your Platonism, Jack. You should
study Aquinas more; you don't really appreciate the
psychosomatic unity.

LEWIS: You're probably right. If I could wrap my
mind around exactly what he means by "matter" and
"form" and "substance"—especially "substance"—I
think I'd understand the Eucharist better. You've got
to try to teach me sometime, Tollers.

TOLKIEN: Not me. I'm no philosopher. Ask Austin.

LEWIS: Oh, I have. And he's a fine teacher. I'm just a
slow student.

GRAHAM: Who's Austin?

LEWIS: Austin Farrer, the best theologian I know. But
look here, we should be talking less about each other
and other people and more about Christ. Can we get
back to the Eucharist?

GRAHAM: Yes, please.

6

Lewis' Faith Defended
against Materialism and Magic

GRAHAM: To be very candid about it, Jack, I sometimes feel a deep suspicion, which I hope is unjustified, that your sacramental theology is close to a kind of pagan magic; that your Eucharist is, to put it very crudely, a kind of mechanical machine, a "Jesus machine". As if the Eucharist were a kind of supernatural vending machine and as if Christ were the bottle of soda pop that it gave us when we put in the correct coin.

LEWIS: The coin being faith?

GRAHAM: Yes. As if faith is reduced to the coin you pay to get the product. That's of course a horrible and unfair caricature, but I suspect your theology sails a little too close to that shore. If I'm a little too close to Scylla, I think you're too close to Charybdis. You see me as too close to Zwingli, but I see you as too close to paganism.

LEWIS: You are more well-versed in the classics than most people suspect, Billy. And I think I do understand your suspicion; I see why that's the way it looks to you. Well, it certainly doesn't look or feel that way to me—either materialistic or magic or a machine. Let's take each of those three objections, or suspicions, one by one, and let me try to tell you, as clearly and honestly as I can, just what I do believe—about our Lord's Real Presence in the Eucharist—by contrasting it with those three misunderstandings, which I don't believe.

GRAHAM: Thank you. That is exactly what I want to hear.

LEWIS: Well, for one thing it's certainly not mechanical or automatic. That's very clear for two reasons.

First, the Church has always forbidden any sacrament to be given without free consent. If the sacraments worked automatically, she'd just send spies to baptize every baby in the world and send them to Heaven. She has always forbidden that and invalidated unfree baptisms. Even infant Baptisms require the free consent of the parents, because the baby can't give it yet.

The second reason is that the Church has always taught that even though the sacraments work *ex opere operato*—from the working of the divine Persons who work in it rather than from the human persons on whom they work—yet the sacraments "work" *on us* only if we have faith, and faith is a free choice of the will, and not an automatic or mechanical thing at all. Even though I believe that faith is a gift of God—as you do, too—I also believe that we are free to refuse the gift. I don't believe in a kind of Calvinistic predestination that takes away free will. The principle I think is crucial here is that God's grace doesn't bypass or take away our human nature, including our free will, which is an essential part of our human nature, but works through it, inspires it, uses it, perfects it. God's grace turns it on, not off.

GRAHAM: Do you believe in predestination too?

LEWIS: Yes.

GRAHAM: Why?

LEWIS: It's in the Bible, for one thing.

GRAHAM: Good. And what about the total sovereignty of God?

LEWIS: That, too. That's in the Bible too, not just in Calvin. But I don't draw the consequences that Calvin draws from it. (And Luther, too, I think.) I don't deny free will.

GRAHAM: I agree with you. I'm more Baptist than Calvinist there. I don't deny free will. But I suspect that Calvin only meant to deny our free will to save ourselves, not all kinds of free will. He certainly believed we were responsible for our choices. I'm not sure about Calvin. But I don't like to oppose those two ideas, predestination and free will. I think both are true, though I don't claim to understand or explain in human terms how that works.

LEWIS: If you had to choose to prioritize one, which would it be?

GRAHAM: In terms of practical importance for us, free will. In terms of priority in time, God's sovereign grace comes first.

LEWIS: I agree with you there. I think we both want to reconcile those two ideas, not simply choose either one over the other. Like Augustine, whom both Protestants and Catholics love to quote selectively.

GRAHAM: I do believe, with the Baptists, that we have to have free will, or free choice, because if we didn't, we couldn't be responsible. But I also believe, with the Calvinists, that God is sovereign, because if He isn't, then He's not God.

LEWIS: So how do you fit them both into the same picture of what really happens? How do you see it working not just in the abstract but in the concrete —not just in the head but in the knees, when we pray for something?

GRAHAM: The only way I can see to answer that question is to say that God's grace comes first—He not only answers our prayers, but He inspires us to pray in the first place—but our free will also comes in, although it comes in second. We pray, not to change God's will, but to fulfill it.

LEWIS: I agree. In *causality*, He's got to be prior. He's the First Cause. But if He's eternal and timeless, it's not a priority in *time*.

GRAHAM: I don't claim to understand that. But I know this: whether it's in time or not, divine grace has to come first. Because if grace is grace, it's not merited. That would be justice. We don't deserve grace. That's why it's called grace, not justice.

And here's another reason: If God is God, and not just *a* god, then He is absolutely sovereign. His actions can't be dependent on ours. God doesn't have to wait to see whether we will choose to accept the grace and then make His decision on that basis. His grace can't depend on our response because He does not depend on us, we depend on Him.

LEWIS: I believe that, too. And I also believe that what happens after that first grace acts on us, or rather *because* that first grace acts on us—what happens when we have His grace in us and then *act* out of faith and love—this happens by both grace and free will, as a baby happens only when a man fertilizes a woman, when the parents combine.

GUY: So we're all women to God.

LEWIS: That's what the mystics say.

GUY: Sounds like a theology of male chauvinism.

LEWIS: If anything, it's an anthropology of female chauvinism.

GRAHAM: I'm not sure how far you can take that analogy, but the principle sounds right to me.

LEWIS: Of course, "all analogies limp", but they get somewhere, at least. I think the principle is that the answer to this question—like most great theological questions—is a both-and, not an either-or.

I don't claim to know how grace works, either, but I can't believe that it's like a single divine puppet master pulling all the many strings on a marionette or like a chain of dominoes, where only the fall of the first domino happens freely because the finger that pushes it is part of a person, who has free will, but all the subsequent dominoes fall automatically and not freely. Rather, I believe that it's like a novel: the characters' actions in the story are both predestined, by the author, and freely chosen, by the characters. They're the actions of persons, not the actions of minerals or machines. Every good story somehow reconciles both predestination and free will.

GRAHAM: I believe that, too. I agree with Augustine that both predestination and free will are real. It's a great mystery, and I don't think we can ultimately understand how they fit together, but both ideas are (to my mind, anyway) pretty clearly taught in the Bible.

LEWIS: So it's clear that the grace of the Sacrament, like all grace, is not mechanical and unfree. Grace is a gift, and a gift has to be freely given *and* freely received. That's the only reason why Hell is possible. If we were forced into Heaven against our will, it wouldn't be a gift but a punishment.

GRAHAM: Agreed.

LEWIS: Your second objection was that my theology made the Eucharist "materialistic". But materialism doesn't mean the affirmation of matter; it means the denial of spirit. And that's certainly not my view. Man is both matter and spirit, both body and soul, and God works His grace on both. The Sacrament is certainly material, but it's also spiritual. It's material, like all sacraments, but not materialistic.

GRAHAM: Oh, I agree there, too. But I still think there's something to my suspicion that your thinking is too close to materialism somehow. I guess what I mean there is really that it looks too much like magic to me.

LEWIS: What do you mean by magic? We agreed that it doesn't work unfreely, without our will, as magic does. Magic is mechanical. It's primitive technology, or preternatural technology.

GRAHAM: That's the heart of my objection, I think: that in your view the sacraments work like machines. Not natural machines, but supernatural machines, but still machines. Not purely material machines, but still machines. Magic. Supernatural machines.

LEWIS: But I just said that they *don't* work that way.

GRAHAM: But you believe that the sacraments work *ex opere operato*, don't you? Isn't that the formula? And doesn't that mean that the thing works by itself rather than through our souls, our spirits, and our free will?

LEWIS: That's the Roman Catholic formula, yes, *ex opere operato* . . .

GRAHAM: So you don't accept that?

LEWIS: I do. At least I accept what I think it means. The sacrament does not work merely through our action, from inside out, so to speak, but from itself, from outside in, by God's power, not ours. In other words, it's not *only* spiritual and subjective but also objective and material: it works through its very matter. The power of its matter works not just on our bodies but also on our souls. Of course it's God who is the first cause of it all, but He uses matter to work on us in the sacraments.

GRAHAM: How do you believe the sacraments work differently from how the Bible works?

LEWIS: They're both from God, gifts of God, and instruments of God for us, of course. But when we read the Bible, the material element is minimal. We could just remember and think of a verse, and it would give us the same grace as when we physically read the black ink on the white paper. But just remembering or thinking of the Sacrament or remembering Christ and His death on the Cross is not the same as receiving the Sacrament physically. The grace works on us physically.

GRAHAM: So if the communion wafer is not eaten, or if the wine is not drunk, we do not get the grace?

LEWIS: Yes, that's right.

GRAHAM: Do you believe that Christ's Blood shed for us on the Cross saves us from our sins?

LEWIS: Yes. That's very clearly taught in the Bible— although how it works, how the "atonement" works, I do not claim to know.

GRAHAM: So it's not anyone else's blood, not the blood of goats and lambs or even the blood of a martyr, that saves us?

LEWIS: Yes, I believe that.

GRAHAM: And that Blood is literal and physical and is really shed in Christ's death?

LEWIS: Yes.

GRAHAM: And you believe you receive that Blood in Holy Communion?

LEWIS: Yes. Holy Communion is one of the ways in which He gets His salvation to us. He is like water to a man dying of thirst (He calls Himself the "living water"), and the sacraments are like hoses, and our reception is like drinking the water from the hose.

GRAHAM: So if you were there two thousand years ago under the Cross when Christ died, and you received His Blood physically, in faith, it would literally save you?

LEWIS: Yes.

GRAHAM: Well, suppose you stood under the wrong cross and received the blood of the Good Thief, instead. Would that save you?

LEWIS: No.

GRAHAM: Not even if you had faith in Christ?

LEWIS: No. Only His Blood saves me, not the Good Thief's.

GRAHAM: But don't you think your faith alone would save you, as it did the Good Thief?

LEWIS: Of course.

GRAHAM: Then it's faith alone that saves you.

LEWIS: No, that does not necessarily follow. God can use many different hoses, so to speak, to get the living water into me. Some are physical, like the sacraments, and some are spiritual, like faith.

GRAHAM: But if you stood under Christ's Cross and received his Blood and had faith, you would be saved.

LEWIS: Yes.

GRAHAM: And if you stood there under Christ's Cross and received His Blood and did not have faith, you would not be saved.

LEWIS: Yes. That's a good way of putting my point that the sacrament is not magic.

GRAHAM: Then it must be just the faith element that saves you when you stand under His Cross and receive His Blood in faith.

LEWIS: No, that does not follow.

GRAHAM: But it does. It's good logic. If you get a reaction from a compound only when a certain element is in it, and you don't get that reaction when that element is not in it, and if you can get that reaction from the element alone when it's not in the compound, then it logically follows that it's that element only that gives you the reaction, not the whole compound.

LEWIS: That sounds like a good analogy, but it's not, because what's missing in that analogy of the chemicals is that in salvation, unlike chemistry, there are two dimensions, the objective and the subjective.

GRAHAM: Matter and spirit, you mean?

LEWIS: No, I mean God and man, grace and free will.

GRAHAM: But those two are not equal. You yourself said that grace is the first cause even of our free choice, though it doesn't take away our free choice. How did you put it?—it turns freedom on, not off.

LEWIS: That's true, they're not *equal*. But they're both *necessary*, because God won't force salvation on you against your will. That's the only reason there's a Hell. Salvation is a gift, but a gift isn't a gift if it isn't freely given, and it's also not a gift if it's not freely received. If I freely give you a slap in the face that you don't want, it's not a gift.

GRAHAM: So faith is our free response to God's gift, our "yes" to the gift.

LEWIS: Yes. We can't do it without Him, and He won't do it without us, without that free response.

GRAHAM: All right, that solves the problem of grace and free will—we need both to be saved—but it doesn't solve the problem of faith and sacraments.

LEWIS: It does if sacraments are what I believe they are: means that God instituted by which He does His part in saving us, means of getting the gift of Christ's life to us—what I called the objective dimension of salvation. Our faith is the subjective dimension.

GRAHAM: But you admitted that He can save us without the sacraments. The Cross is sufficient as the objective dimension, and our faith is sufficient as the subjective dimension.

LEWIS: Yes, I agree with that, too. But just as faith alone without good works can save us in an extraordinary situation like that of the Good Thief, so also the Cross alone without the sacraments can save us in the extraordinary situation of Protestantism, where you don't believe in His Real Presence in the sacraments. But just as objective good works are the ordinary and expected result of subjective faith, so the objective sacraments He instituted are the ordinary means He uses to get His life into us if we have the subjective faith to receive it.

GRAHAM: So are you saying that Protestantism is as exceptional a case as that of the Good Thief?

LEWIS: Obviously not in one sense: there was only one such Good Thief, and there are only a very few people who die right after conversion, as he did, so that they have no time for any good works; but there are millions of Protestants who believe in the saving power of faith alone and not the sacraments. So your "back door", so to speak, is a lot larger than his. But in another sense, yes, the Good Thief and Protestants are similar because they're both back doors, not the ordinary, God-intended front door.

GRAHAM [laughing]: So you're calling us Protestants good thieves, sneaking into the heavenly house by the back door?

LEWIS [also laughing]: Isn't there a verse about that in the Gospels, about the Kingdom of Heaven being taken by violence?

GRAHAM: Jack, I frankly feel confused about you. We've just agreed about almost every principle, and yet I still get the strong feeling that what you believe is too much like magic. In fact, I think that's my major objection. I wish I could make it more clear, but it's a strong feeling or suspicion that I can't ignore.

LEWIS: Then we have to keep hammering at that issue until we do get it clear.

GRAHAM: I couldn't find anything in any of your writings about the sacraments, though. Why didn't you ever write about that, as the Roman Catholics do, if what you believe is essentially the same as what they believe about it?[1]

LEWIS: I'm not sure that I do believe all that they believe about the Sacrament. But the reason I never wrote about it is very simple: I have nothing to say. I'm not a theologian. I don't claim to understand it much better than the ordinary layman does.[2]

But I do see something that I think is crucially important to answer your objection about magic. Like Tollers, I would make a sharp distinction between two very different kinds of magic, and I think you are confusing the two. Tollers said something like that in *The Lord of the Rings*, in distinguishing the magic of the Elves and the magic of Sauron's Ring —isn't that right, Tollers? Isn't the conflict in that book a conflict between those two opposite kinds of magic?[3]

TOLKIEN: It is indeed. The Ring, or those who use it, exemplify one kind of magic, and the Elves exemplify

---

[1] Actually, Lewis did address the question of "magic" in his last full-length book, *Letters to Malcolm: Chiefly on Prayer* (reissued: San Francisco: HarperOne, 2017), p. 9, where he wrote: "My ideas about the sacrament would probably be called 'magical' by a good many modern theologians."

[2] This also comes out in *Letters to Malcolm*, when Lewis writes: "You ask me why I've never written anything about the Holy Communion. For the very simple reason that I am not good enough at Theology. I have nothing to offer." Ibid., p. 136.

[3] Once again, Lewis wrote later about this more explicitly, in *Letters to Malcolm*: "When I say 'magic' I am not thinking of the paltry

the other. The first is power, and the second is enchantment. The first comes from below, and the second comes from above. Technology uses power, and good art uses enchantment, and they are not only different but opposite.

GRAHAM: How?

TOLKIEN: The first is a war against nature, an insistence on making it change to conform to our will. The second is a love of nature and a desire to augment it and glorify it and a desire to conform to it, as an artist conforms to the beauty he sees and creates, and to glorify it, to show others the joy of that conforming. I think that's pretty much what the Psalmists meant by "praise" when they keep praising the Lord. That's also pretty much what I mean by "enchantment" or "Faerie", as I put it in my essay on fairy stories. In fact, I wrote there somewhere . . . no, Jack, don't look for the book, I don't need it, I have it in my memory . . . "Faerie (the realm of fairy tales) itself may perhaps most nearly be translated by Magic—but it is magic of a peculiar mood and power, at the furthest pole from the vulgar devices of the laborious, scientific magician."

GRAHAM: So your book is an attack on technology?

TOLKIEN: No, on technologism, on making technology the whole or primary meaning of life. *The Lord*

---

and pathetic techniques by which fools attempt and quacks pretend to control Nature. I mean rather what is suggested by fairy-tale sentences like . . . : 'This is a magic cave and those who enter it will renew their youth.'" Ibid., p. 139.

of the Rings has a lot of good technology in it as well as bad—swords, cities, boats. As our world does, too.

LEWIS: I made a similar point in my book *The Abolition of Man* when I pointed out that magic (the bad magic) and technology (or rather technologism) arose at the same time: not in the Middle Ages, but in the Renaissance. Because both are essentially the same thing, the same philosophy, the same goal: not to be conquered by the beauty or meaning or value of nature—that's what Tollers calls "enchantment"—but to conquer nature. Magic was tried first, before technology, because it was easier. But it didn't work, so they turned to technology, instead. But the two have the same purpose. As I said in that book, this is the essence of the difference between modern Western civilization and the Christian civilization that preceded it in the Middle Ages. Francis Bacon trumpets that new meaning of life: to conform nature to man, not man to the nature of things.

GRAHAM: You don't mean a kind of fatalism, do you, by "the nature of things"?

LEWIS: No, no, I mean the nature of God, first of all, and then the nature of morality, the "natural" law, and then the nature of creatures, treating humans like humans, not like either gods or animals.

GRAHAM: That makes a lot of sense.

LEWIS: As I wrote there, to our ancestors, the primary problem of human life was to conform our souls, our minds and desires, to nature in that sense, to the nature of things; and the means for doing that were wisdom and virtue, especially the four cardinal virtues and the three theological virtues, faith and hope and charity. But for magic and technology alike, the primary problem of human life was how to make nature conform to our own souls, our own wills, our own desires; and the method was applied science, the machine, power, force—the Ring.

GRAHAM: I see. So when you say our ancestors tried to conform their souls to nature, or to the nature of things, what you mean by "the nature of things" is first of all God.

LEWIS: Yes.

GRAHAM: How do you relate that to conforming to God's creation?

LEWIS: I suppose I should say that we conform to God's mind and will absolutely and to nature relatively, insofar as nature is God's art and reflects the Artist. I call it "patches of Godlight" falling on the woods of our experience. And I don't mean just material things like woods. I'd include our reason and the natural moral law as aspects of nature, or of God's design in nature, especially in our human nature.

GRAHAM: But how does this distinction between the two magics apply to the Eucharist? That's neither art nor technology. Neither art nor technology works *ex opere operato*, as you believe the Eucharist does. Why is the Sacrament like art, or like what you and Tolkien call the good magic?

LEWIS: Good question. I didn't make that clear yet, did I? Well, let's try this example. Let's say you are reading a fairy tale, and the author writes: "This is a magic cave, and if you enter it, it will renew your youth."

GRAHAM: Are you saying that the sacraments are like magic caves?

LEWIS: In an important way, yes. It is a supernatural magic that works on our souls, if we choose to let it, as the beauty of nature is a kind of natural magic that works on our souls, too. I'm told an American Indian tribe (I think it's the Iroquois) have a word for that magical power nature has over our souls. The word is *orenda*. And the magic in nature and the magic in the sacraments both get into our souls through our bodies, unlike faith. Technology works only materially, and faith works only spiritually, but both the good magic of *orenda* and the sacraments work in both ways at the same time.

GRAHAM: Sorry, but it's still not clear to me.

LEWIS: Perhaps it's not quite clear enough in my own mind, either. Let's see whether an example will help. Go back to the one Tollers wrote about. The bad kind of magic is exemplified by Sauron's Ring, and by the Ring of Gyges in Plato's *Republic*, which is the model for Sauron's Ring once it falls into the hands of Gollum. Gollum is almost exactly like Gyges.

TOLKIEN: Here, let me quote from one of my letters to try to explain the difference. When I said in the essay on fairy stories that the bad magic was the magic of "the laborious, scientific magician", I had in mind technologism, what Bacon called "man's conquest of nature". Here is how I put it in one of my letters. It is "a magic of external plans or devices (apparatus) instead of development of the inherent inner powers or talents . . . bulldozing the real world, or coercing other wills. The Machine is our more obvious modern form. . . . I have not used 'magic' consistently, and indeed the Elven-queen Galadriel is obliged to remonstrate with the Hobbits on their confused use of the word both for the devices and operations of the Enemy, and for those of the Elves . . . the Elves are there [in my, tales] to demonstrate the difference. Their 'magic' is Art . . . not Power."

GRAHAM: Are you saying that art can save you?

TOLKIEN: Of course not. I'm saying that the sacraments work more as art works rather than as technology works. They work by enchantment.

GRAHAM: So if you're not enchanted, you're not religious?

TOLKIEN: No, I don't mean the ordinary kind of enchantment.

GRAHAM: You're talking about the Eucharist now, right?

TOLKIEN: Yes, but not only there.

GRAHAM: In all your seven sacraments, then?

TOLKIEN: Yes, but more than that: in general, too, in the heart of religion.

GRAHAM: What do you mean by "the heart of religion"?

TOLKIEN: I believe Muslims call it *islam*, or surrender. Surrender to God.

GRAHAM: I'm still a bit foggy on what you mean.

LEWIS: Let me try to explain it to you, Billy. I think you'd agree, wouldn't you, that the essence of religion is not conquering the world, or, certainly, conquering God (which is of course impossible), but letting God conquer you, right?

GRAHAM: Of course.

LEWIS: That's why the Muslims call it "surrender". It means entering the holy city on your knees, conforming to God's will in your life, especially in your moral choices, especially by agape love, and also conforming to God's mind as He revealed it to you in the Bible and in the Church by believing what He revealed there and also in His other book, nature and natural reason. And there's a third conformity, conforming to God's heart by admiring the beauty He created for you in physical nature and that He inspired for you in great art. You see, love, faith, and hope, the three greatest things in the world, pretty much correspond to goodness, truth, and beauty, three attributes of God, and to our will, our mind, and our heart, three attributes of the image of God in us.

Magic is a kind of power. What Tollers calls "Faerie" and "Enchantment" and "Art" and "Elvish magic" —four names for the same thing—this has an inner power, a spiritual, personal power. Technology has the opposite kind of power: external, physical, impersonal, mechanical power, coercive force over things and over human bodies and even over human souls by psychological manipulation or manipulative propaganda or by political totalitarianism, either the hard kind, like Orwell's *1984*, or the soft kind, like Huxley's *Brave New World*. Our age is full of all those kinds of technological power. We're a lot like Tollers' Sauron—which is why we never see his face in *The Lord of the Rings*: because it's our own face.

That kind of magic is the might that pretends to make its own right. The other kind of magic is the right that makes its own might. The Chinese call it *te*, the spiritual power of a wise and holy human soul that freely influences other souls. It's a spiritual gravity, the power of the good to attract good men.

I've been lecturing. Sorry. Do you see a little of what we mean?

GRAHAM: I think so. I see the contrast pretty clearly if I remember Plato's *Republic* and contrast Gyges with Socrates.

LEWIS: Exactly! It's all in Plato, all in Plato. Bless me, what *do* they teach them at these schools?

GRAHAM: And I understand the notion of *te*, or spiritual power. But that's how *I* see the sacraments: as spiritual, not physical. I thought you believed the sacraments work *ex opere operato*, as the Catholics teach. That would be the physical magic, the machine, the supernatural technology.

TOLKIEN: We Catholics don't see it as merely physical. The chemical and physical appearances of the bread and wine remain unchanged after the consecration in the Eucharist. It's not technology.

GRAHAM: Then why do you call it *ex opere operato*?

TOLKIEN: Because the power, the spiritual power, is from God, not from us.

GRAHAM: Oh. Then it's almost another term for divine grace.

TOLKIEN: Yes. Grace is a gift. When I give you a gift, it doesn't come from you, or from your faith or your love or your worthiness, but from me, from my love. It comes to you *ex opere operato*, which means literally "from the working of the one who is doing the work", which is me, the giver, not you, the receiver. And in the case of the sacraments, that's God, not man. That's why it's not magic. It's a personal gift, not a mechanical machine.

GRAHAM: I see. Whether your theology is true or false, at least it's not pagan magic, as I feared.

TOLKIEN: It's Our Lord personally offering to you His own person, the whole of Him, which is both divine and human, and within the human both the body and soul, and within the body both the flesh and the shed blood.

GRAHAM: Do you buy all that, Jack?

LEWIS: Well, I do believe in the Real Presence of Our Lord in the Eucharist, and I do not see how I can subtract anything from what Tollers just said: the divinity or the humanity, the body or the soul, the flesh or the blood. But I do not claim to understand what the Catholic dogma of Transubstantiation really means, so I must confess agnosticism about that. And since I do not believe I am under the authority of Rome, I do not think I have to believe it on that authority alone. So I do not think I would be a heretic if I said that Transubstantiation is not a dogma but merely a permissible philosophical and theological opinion, or, as the Orthodox call it, a theologoumenon. It's like the relation between the Atonement itself versus any theory of the Atonement: the Atonement is a dogma, but Augustine's theory of how it works, or Anselm's, or Aquinas', or Luther's, is only an alternative possible explanation. So I think that those are the two points where I do not go as far as the Catholics go: the necessity of the formula of Transubstantiation and the authority of the Church that supports it. But the Real Presence, yes indeed, with all my heart I do believe it, just as Tollers does.

GRAHAM: But you do not regard it as magical in the sense of impersonal or automatic or necessary, like a machine.

LEWIS: No, but neither do Roman Catholics, like Tollers, if they understand their faith well rather than superstitiously.

GUY: So to whom are you closer on the Eucharist? To Billy or to Tolkien?

LEWIS: Oh, I think that has to be Tollers.

GUY: Why?

LEWIS: Look at it this way. Suppose a Roman Catholic is as superstitious and as pagan and as materialistic and as "magical" as you suspect he is. He is making a serious mistake about the Real Presence. He is thinking that it is physical and chemical. And let's say that that is indeed a simple-minded and even stupid mistake. But is there not also an opposite and worse mistake?—thinking that since the Presence is not physical, it must be merely spiritual and thinking that *that* means it must be not objective but subjective and personal and dependent on your faith; that what's really there is not Christ but only a holy symbol of Christ—which is what most Protestants believe.

GRAHAM: So your point is a kind of Pascal's wager? That it's safer to risk the smaller mistake? The first one, the superstition? If you say that, you're *assuming* that the first mistake is the smaller one. You don't prove it.

LEWIS: That's true, but that's not my point. My point is simply to answer your question about which of these two views is farther from mine. I think yours is. For the simple-minded and superstitious Catholic at least believes in the Real Presence, even though he doesn't understand it properly. Isn't that the most important question—who or what is there? Is He really present? Is that really Christ, or is it only a symbol? Surely the difference between those two things— the incarnate God and a symbol—is infinitely greater than the difference between the most correct possible understanding of that presence and the most stupid and superstitious misunderstanding of it.

GUY: If you're right, then the difference between some Protestants and others, between Protestants who don't believe in the Real Presence (like me) and Protestants who do (like Lutherans and Anglicans) is much greater than the difference between those

Anglican or Lutheran Protestants and Roman Catholics.

LEWIS: Yes. By the way, we Anglicans don't call ourselves Protestants *or* Roman Catholics.

TOLKIEN [explaining to Billy and Guy]: It's their so-called *via media*. Anglicans are stuck in the middle of the Tiber, with both feet on neither bank.

GRAHAM: Let me see if I can sort all this out. Let me try to summarize what we've just gone through. Please be patient with me, because my mind doesn't work as quickly as yours on that level of abstraction.

At first, the two of you, Jack and Tollers, seemed to distinguish just *two* views of the Eucharist. You two, both you Anglicans and you Roman Catholics, believe that Christ is really present in the Sacrament, in the bread and wine or along with the bread and wine or, rather, instead of the bread and wine. (At least I got it right the third time.) And most Protestants, like myself and Guy, say that's not true: He is really present in our souls but only symbolically present in the Sacrament, in the bread and wine. Then Jack tried to stake out a third view, a *via media*, which seems to me pretty much the same as the Catholic view. But it gets much more complicated if you bring in the Lutheran view and the Calvinist view and others that they fought about around the time of the Reformation.

LEWIS: Yes.

GUY: And we're still fighting.

LEWIS: Yes, but only in words, not in wars. And we're also listening to each other. And we're trying to love each other and emphasize what we have in common much more than what we don't. And those are, I think, three very large pieces of progress.

GRAHAM: I think we all agree there.

7

Other Possible Positions:
Compromises?

GUY: What about those other positions, though? Can you tell us about them, Jack? I think I underestimated now many very different positions there were among Protestants.

LEWIS: All right, but it will have to be pretty short and simple. I'm neither a professional historian nor a professional theologian, but I think I know enough about that period to try to distinguish three different Protestant positions at that time. What they all have in common is that they disagree with the Catholic position, which is Transubstantiation, which means that the whole substance or essence or being of the bread and wine ceases to exist and becomes the literal Body and Blood of Christ. Only the appearances of bread and wine remain, as a kind of disguise that He hides behind.

GUY: So, according to this Catholic position, since anyone's body and blood are physical, it's a physical presence.

TOLKIEN: Sorry, but I need to correct that. It's the presence of His Body, but it's not a physical and chemical change that happens. Put a consecrated Host under a microscope and it looks exactly like ordinary unleavened bread. Science perceives only the appearances, and the appearances don't change.

GRAHAM: I don't understand your distinction between bodily presence and physical and chemical presence. Bodies are physical and chemical, aren't they?

TOLKIEN: It's a change, not in the appearances, but in the substance, the essential being. Physics and chemistry tell us about appearances. They don't tell us what is the substance.

LEWIS: Frankly, Tollers, I never understood that. What is "substance"? When I try to think that concept, my mind comes up with something like a grey clay or plastic that changes color and shape.

TOLKIEN: That's not your mind, that's your imagination.

LEWIS: I accept your correction and your distinction. But my mind simply cannot wrap itself around the concept of "substance".

TOLKIEN [half-jokingly]: In that case, perhaps it is a piece of providential good fortune that you did not get the job you wanted at Oxford, in philosophy instead of literature.

GRAHAM: Can we define the different views?

LEWIS: Yes, let's. There's the Roman Catholic view, and there's my Anglican view, which is close to it, and then there were at least three main Protestant views at the time of the Reformation: Luther's, Zwingli's, and Calvin's.

Luther's view denies Transubstantiation but affirms what he calls Consubstantiation. That means that Christ is really present, objectively and personally, there in the sacrament, behind the disguise of bread and wine, but the bread and wine remain bread and wine, they don't get transubstantiated, they don't disappear in reality, or in essence, or in substance, any more than they disappear in appearance.

Zwingli totally disagreed with that and saw it as the same superstitious and idolatrous error as the Roman view. He said the presence was only symbolic. In fact, he called Luther's view demonic, from the devil. And Luther famously responded, "One of our positions comes from God and one comes from the devil, and I do not get my theology from the devil." When he was asked what he meant by the Real Presence and how it was different from Zwingli's, he took a knife and stabbed a table with it (he was very big and strong and stout) and said, *"That's* what I mean."

Then Calvin tried to mediate between the two, but he succeeded only in exacerbating the polemics in creating a new, third position.

GRAHAM: What was his position?

LEWIS: I don't understand it well at all, but I know he calls the Sacrament "a sign and a seal", not just a sign. He's not a Zwinglian. He says we actually receive grace through it, and grace comes from God, so God is present there, objectively present, all three Persons, Father, Son, and Holy Spirit, sealing His people with His name, really doing something and not just signifying something with a symbol. But it's not Luther's version of Real Presence.

TOLKIEN: I never knew Calvin said that. I thought he simply denied the Real Presence altogether.

GUY: I know Calvin a little. I think he means that Christ is really present in us when we receive Holy Communion and gives us a special grace, but He is present, not objectively, in the material elements of the Sacrament, but only in our souls. It's a spiritual presence.

TOLKIEN: It's subjective, then.

GUY: No, not if you mean that it's in our imagination or fantasy or feeling, or *from* them. It's grace, so it's from God.

TOLKIEN: So it's spiritual but not subjective?

GUY: He doesn't use those terms, but I think that's what he means. The grace is in our souls, but it's not *from* our souls.

LEWIS: And which view is yours, Billy, now that we've distinguished them?

GRAHAM: As I said, I'm not a theologian. I suppose I would agree more with Calvin on this issue, even though I'm not a Calvinist in other ways. Most Baptists are suspicious of Calvin and Calvinism.

LEWIS: One thing this unclear controversy teaches us clearly is that "presence" is not as clear and simple a concept as we think.

GUY: What do you mean? It's either physical or spiritual, isn't it?

LEWIS: Well, let's see. Suppose you say it's spiritual and mental and subjective. Suppose I believe in your existence and I love you very much, and I'm thinking clearly and consciously and passionately about you, but you are on a rocket ship halfway to the moon, not even on the earth. Are you really present to me?

GUY: Obviously not. So I suppose that for us bodily creatures, presence has to be physical.

LEWIS: But suppose I accidentally knock you down in a crowd, and I see you down there on the ground, and I apologize, and I extend my hand to pick you up, but I don't see your face. You're just another anonymous walker that I happened to bump into. Are you really present to me?

GUY: No. That's a puzzle: presence seems neither spiritual nor physical. I guess it must be both.

LEWIS: But suppose that at the very moment I accidentally knock you down, I also happen to be thinking about you, and I know you and love you, but I don't know that it's you I just knocked down. Are we present to each other?

GUY: No.

LEWIS: So even though we each have a body and a soul, we can't be present to each other simply in a bodily way or simply in a mental way (intellectual or volitional or emotional or all three) or simply in both ways at once.

GUY: So what is presence, then?

LEWIS: It has to be personal, doesn't it? The person, the "I" that *has* this body and this soul, has to be present to the other person.

GRAHAM: That sounds more like spiritual presence than bodily presence.

LEWIS: They can't be separated—body and spirit, or body and soul—they aren't separated at any moment in life. Only death separates them. Life does not. That's why we can't separate them when we are really and fully present to each other. And that's why we can't separate them in the Eucharist, either. And that's one of the reasons why I believe Christ is also bodily present there, present in His Body and with His Body. He did institute it by saying "This is My Body", after all!

GRAHAM: Which could mean "this symbolizes My Body." He didn't specify how to interpret it.

TOLKIEN: Yes, He did.

GRAHAM: Where?

TOLKIEN: In John 6. When He said that we had to eat His body and drink His blood, and most of his disciples were so scandalized that they left Him then and there, He didn't call them back and correct them and say, "Don't be so materialistic. I didn't mean it literally. It's only a symbol."

GUY: So you're saying that Billy doesn't know his Bible?

GRAHAM: Oh, I think I'm not denying anything in the Bible. In fact, I can honestly say that I believe in His real presence, too, though not in exactly the same way as you do, because the Bible does clearly teach it, but it doesn't limit it to the Eucharist. He Himself said, "Where two or three are gathered in

My name, there am I in the midst of them." "There am I"—that certainly means presence, doesn't it?

LEWIS: Certainly. But that's not the same kind of presence as the disciples had before He physically ascended into Heaven. And it's not the same kind of presence as in the Eucharist. When two or three, or two or three thousand, are gathered in His name, in a church, He is present; but when we celebrate the Eucharist, something else, some kind of new presence, is added. Otherwise, it would be superfluous to celebrate the Eucharist; it would add nothing to what we had before, when we had only prayer and worship. The first presence, to His disciples before His Ascension, was physical; His presence when we gather to worship is spiritual, in our souls; and the third kind of presence, when we celebrate the Eucharist, is different from both of the other two because it's sacramental. It's the same Person who's present, but it's three different kinds of presence.

GRAHAM: So He is really present in all three ways but differently.

LEWIS: Yes, and in more than those three ways. I think we can expand the list of different ways He is present.

GRAHAM: How?

LEWIS: Well, let's see. As the Word of God who was the instrument by whom God created the world, Christ is present in all creation, in every atom. But within the creation, He is not as present in lifeless things as He is in living things, since God is life in the highest degree. And He is not as present in plant life as He is in animal life, since animals have feelings and love on a low level, instinctive affection, and some kind of consciousness and intelligence, as plants don't. And He is not present in any other animal as He is in man, who has a spiritual soul that has reason and conscience and free will. And He is not as present in an evil man as He is in a good man, and he is not as present in an unbeliever, who has only natural human life, as He is in a believer, who has supernatural life, eternal life. And He is more present when two or three believers are gathered than He is when there is only one—more present in even the most rudimentary church than in any of its individuals. And He is still more present when the sacraments are administered than when they are not. Finally, He is not as fully present in any of the other sacraments as in the Eucharist, where He is present in His Body and Blood.

GRAHAM: Do you say that you worship the Eucharist, then?

LEWIS: I worship Him, and Him alone. But I believe He is really present there, so I worship Him there, as His Church has done from the beginning.

GRAHAM: You believe He is hiding behind the appearances, as a spy would hide behind a mask?

LEWIS: Yes. Truly there, hiding. But not just passively. Acting. Hiding is an act.

GRAHAM: But really there, as really as He was there on the dusty streets of Jerusalem two thousand years ago.

LEWIS: Yes.

GRAHAM: I think that is the line in the sand that I cannot cross. I can go as far as Calvin, but no farther.

LEWIS: I think that is indeed the line in the sand— the most important dividing line, anyway. So now that we've defined the essential difference, are we ready to take the next step, which is to argue about it, to debate it?

GUY: I hope so. What's the point of understanding a belief unless you find out whether it's true or not?

GRAHAM: You're right there, Guy. Truth—that has to be an absolute.

GUY: And arguing and reasoning is at least one way to find truth, isn't it? Isn't that the whole point of reasoning, just as it's the whole point of defining?

LEWIS: You are a good philosopher, Guy! I completely agree with you

GRAHAM: And so do I, and so I consent to the debate, as long as we don't forget we are doing it because we are Christians; we are doing it for Him, not just to win arguments or to satisfy our curiosity.

LEWIS: Thank you for reminding us of that, Billy.

TOLKIEN: But I think we need another break before we start that next step. Are you hungry? I see that you don't automatically say No. We've all been so focused on our words that we've left the crumpets pretty much untouched. I have some sandwiches, enough for all of us, if you'd like them. Yes? Good. Christopher! Bring out the sandwiches, and let's have another hot pot of tea.

And after a significant number of insignificant little sandwiches, they begin their debate.

8

Graham's Faith and
Lewis' Deeper Critique

GRAHAM: I came here for two reasons, Jack: first and foremost, to meet you as a fellow Christian and to thank you for helping so many people find the Way, the Truth, and the Life through your writings. But also I came to meet you to find out what you believe and why you believe it. I didn't come for a debate, but I guess it's time for one now. But I want to make clear before we start that I will participate only if it's a serious search for truth and not just a personal game to win.

LEWIS: That's exactly what a good debate is: a serious search for truth.

GRAHAM: And it has to be a serious topic. And we agreed that the doctrine of the Eucharist was perhaps the most serious and passionate point of disagreement between Protestants like myself and Catholics and Anglo-Catholics like yourself.

LEWIS: Yes.

GRAHAM: So I'm not out to "win" this debate personally. There's nothing personal in it. Or, if there is, it's about the person of Christ and about our personal relationship with Him. So I want to be part of this debate only because for me it's part of getting to know Him better and also getting to know you better and getting to understand where you're coming from, why you believe what you believe.

LEWIS: I understand that, and I appreciate it. But of course a good debate is also a search for truth.

GRAHAM: That's what it should be for those who don't have the truth, or who aren't sure of it, yes, of course. But what if we firmly believe we already know a truth? How can we search for something we have? Did you ever see anyone searching all over for his own head?

LEWIS: Oh, I think you can find some crazy philosopher who does that. In fact, I once wrote a preface to a book by just such a philosopher: D. E. Harding's *The Hierarchy of Heaven and Earth*, which began with his search for his own head. But seriously, even those who believe they already know a certain truth can search for a greater appreciation of it or a better understanding of it or better reasons for it. So we can both do that, I think.

GRAHAM: All right. I guess my concern is that this might be a formal debate instead of an informal conversation among friends. I think your mind is so sharp that you would easily win a formal debate with me by defending any side of any topic at all.

LEWIS: I think you underestimate your own intellect, Billy, and overestimate mine. But OK, I'll try to remember that this is not a formal debate. But it *is* an argument, not just "sharing our feelings".

GRAHAM: Right. I'll try to remember that Scripture commands us to "be ready to give a reason for the hope that is in you."

LEWIS: And I'll try to remember the First Commandment. I think my favorite idol is loving argumentation for its own sake instead of as a mere means to finding the truth. It's the besetting sin of so-called intellectuals.

GRAHAM: Oh, I think we all do that, whether we're intellectuals or not. We just want to outdo each other. But of course two people can't possibly outdo each other at the same time.

LEWIS: It's logically impossible.

GRAHAM: Also morally impossible. I think that's one of the reasons God gave us the moral law: to stop us from pursuing that impossible goal and to get us to love our neighbors as ourselves. Of all the things you've written, the thing I appreciated the most was your chapter on pride in *Mere Christianity*: how it's the greatest sin, and how it's really the sin in every sin, because it sets each of us against the other and against Our Lord.

LEWIS: Well, now that we've both confessed our sins, I hope we can celebrate the rest of our liturgy of argument together. [Polite laughter.] And it's definitely not going to be a formal debate; I'm sure we'll want to wander at will wherever our argument leads us, like a raft on a river. But let's *begin* with the debate format, at least.

So let's formulate our issue: Resolved: that Catholics are committing idolatry by believing in the Real

Presence of Christ in the Eucharist and by Eucharistic adoration.

GRAHAM: But I don't say you are an idolater, either morally or intellectually. I don't think you're either wicked or stupid. I just disagree with your theology, as you disagree with mine.

LEWIS: But if my theology is idolatry, I'm an idolater. I'm worshipping something as God that isn't God.

GRAHAM: But your personal motives may well be very good and honest and honorable and even holy.

LEWIS: But idolatry is a serious *sin*, not just a theological mistake.

GUY: You're right, Jack. God may forgive you for it, but He doesn't just wave His hand and breezily say, "Forget about it, there's nothing to forgive." I think Billy is being nicer to you than God is. In that chapter in *The Great Divorce*, you yourself wrote about the heretical bishop in Hell, that there are sins of the intellect, too.

GRAHAM: That's true, Guy, but remember that the heart of worship is the heart. And I think this man's heart is probably right even if his mind is wrong on this issue. After all, the Apostle Paul didn't add theological correctness to his list of the three greatest things in the world. They were faith, hope, and, above all, charity.

LEWIS: Yes, but truth is essential, too. In fact, in one sense, it's more essential than faith and hope, because Saint Paul says that faith and hope are only for this world of time, but truth, like charity, is eternal. And even in this world, faith and hope are good only if they are the true faith and true hope. False faith and false hope are very harmful.

GRAHAM: I don't disagree with you there. That's why I consented to debate this issue: for the truth. Because it's extremely important to worship the true God, and Him alone. But suppose you think that the true God is in some place where He really isn't, or you think that He isn't in some place where He really is. And suppose you love Him with all your heart, and you want to worship Him wherever He is. Then even if your mind is wrong about where He is, your heart is right about Who He is and why you love Him, and that's what God judges first and foremost. What we differ about is only where He is, whether He is there in the Eucharist, and, if so, just how He is there. Our hearts can be totally united in His love even though our minds are divided about His address.

LEWIS: Of course. I quite agree.

GRAHAM: I don't think that is an "of course". I think that's absolutely crucial for us to acknowledge before we begin to argue about which position is the right one.

LEWIS: I totally agree with you there, too, Billy. And I think Guy does, too.

GUY: I'm not sure. I just can't help feeling that you're just being just a little too . . . too *nice*.

GRAHAM: Look, Guy. Suppose you were the Samaritan woman whom Jesus met and converted in chapter 4 of John's Gospel. And suppose He left your little Samaritan town, and you wanted to find Him and fall at His feet and worship Him and follow Him wherever He went. And suppose he's really in Galilee, which is north of where you are, in Samaria, but you think He's teaching in the Temple in Jerusalem, to the south, so you make a pilgrimage to Jerusalem. Suppose you have to sell everything you have to make that journey, but you do it out of love, out of love for Him. You turn your face to Jerusalem in worship because you think He is there. But even though you're wrong in your mind, you're right in your heart. Now suppose there's another person, a Jew who lives in Galilee, where Jesus now is, and his heart is not set on Jesus at all. Suppose this Jew is not even a sincere truth seeker; he just doesn't care. Jesus is right there in his backyard, and he knows it, but he doesn't care. Which of the two is more pleasing to God?

GUY: Obviously, the Samaritan woman.

GRAHAM: Here's an actual scriptural example. The Apostle Paul, in Acts 17, is preaching to the pagan Greeks in Athens, and he sees all the idols there, the false gods, and he sees one altar dedicated to "the unknown God", so he says, to those Greeks who are sincere enough to admit their ignorance and who are seeking the unknown God, "The God you are already worshipping as unknown [the Greek verb is in the present progressive tense, meaning something habitual] I will now reveal to you." Their hearts were right, even though their minds were wrong. That's not *enough*; good intentions alone are not enough; the Apostle has to tell them the truth about God; but it's a good start.

LEWIS: That "unknown God" was the God Socrates spoke of. I wouldn't be surprised if Socrates himself cut that inscription. His father was a stonecutter, you know.

GRAHAM: Here's another example of my principle, from Kierkegaard. He once wrote something like this: If a pagan goes into a pagan temple to worship the pagan god, with pagan ideas in his mind, but he believes this is the true god, and he worships this false god with all the passion and love of his heart, seeking only to worship the true God, is that not true worship, even though it's ignorant and theologically false? And if a Christian goes into a Christian church, a church that teaches the truth about the true God, but he worships in a false spirit, is there not less truth there, in that worship, than in the pagan's worship?

LEWIS: That's what Kierkegaard means by "truth is subjectivity", isn't it?

GRAHAM: I think so.

LEWIS: I am very suspicious of Kierkegaard because that sounds like relativism and subjectivism to me.

GRAHAM: I don't think so. Someone who knows Kierkegaard better than I do pointed out to me that he is not denying objective truth; in fact, he is presupposing objective truth, but he's saying there's something even more important than that, and he doesn't call that "subjective truth" but "truth as subjectivity". There's a big difference.

LEWIS: What's the difference?

GRAHAM: I think by "subjectivity" he means an honest and passionate personal love and seeking of the one true God, whoever and wherever He may be. If I'm not mistaken, you said something very much like that at the end of the last book in your Narnia series, with Emeth.

GUY: Who's Emeth?

GRAHAM: Emeth is not a Narnian. He doesn't know Aslan, the true God. He's a pagan, a Calormene, who worships a false god, Tash, because he doesn't know any better, and he thinks Tash is the true god. When he dies, he meets Aslan, who judges him, and to his great surprise Aslan accepts Emeth's worship because it's true worship, even though its object is the wrong object, the wrong god. He explains to Emeth that everything true and good belongs to him, Aslan, the true God. So there was a kind of truth in Emeth's worship, even though it's not objective truth. All truth is God's truth. He claims it.

LEWIS: You've interpreted that passage correctly, Billy. In fact, I picked that name, "Emeth", because it's the Hebrew word for truth.

GRAHAM: So it seems to me you are saying there the same thing Kierkegaard is saying!

LEWIS: Again I am "hoisted on my own petard!" You win that one, Billy. I repent of my injustice to Kierkegaard. I don't enjoy reading him—it feels to me like trying to walk through a sandstorm—but that's no proof of falsehood. It might be *true* sand. Perhaps I've read the wrong books about Kierkegaard.

GRAHAM: Books that praise him or books that criticize him?

LEWIS: Both. The modernists praise him for his subjectivism, and the traditionalists blame him for his subjectivism, but perhaps both sides got him wrong there.

GRAHAM: Well, I don't know that for sure. After all, I'm not a professional theologian or philosopher.

LEWIS: That's probably why you *didn't* get him wrong. I trust you more than I trust them.

GUY: Well, whoever is right about Kierkegaard, the point about our argument here is that we both agree with you, Billy, that the heart is more important than the head. But Jack, I still think you're a head-heretic about the Church and Tradition and especially about the Eucharist, even though you're not a heart-heretic. So if God judges hearts more than heads, I don't think you'll burn for it, either in this world or in the next. But you'll be corrected.

LEWIS: Well, that makes me a little more comfortable, and therefore I might even dare to light up my pipe in your presence, if you don't mind.

GUY: I promise I won't burn you at the stake.

LEWIS: The only stakes in this house are what's at stake in the argument. And that's nothing less than the truth.

GUY: Not just abstract truth, but the One who *is* the Truth, and the Way, and the Life.

LEWIS: Should we try to explore what He meant when He said, "I AM the truth"? How Truth can be a Person?

GRAHAM: I'd rather not get into such an abstract philosophical question, if you don't mind. We all believe in objective truth, and we all believe in Christ, so neither truth nor Christ is at issue here in our argument. What's at issue is the Eucharist, whether it's true that He is really present in the Eucharist. And I'm interested in finding out where you're coming from, Jack, what leads you to that belief. Can you tell me your main reason?

LEWIS: Well, now, I suppose if I had honestly to pick just one reason, it would have to be what the Roman Catholics call Tradition. The word "catholic" means "universal", you know, and I am a catholic in that small-c sense, though not in the large-C sense.

GUY: In fact the large-C sense is self-contradictory, because before calling it universal, with the word "Catholic", they call it local and particular, with the word "Roman".

TOLKIEN: Ah, but this particular IS universal—like the Jews.

LEWIS: Let's not get into all that. Let's keep to our focus, shall we?

GRAHAM: Yes, I think we should.

LEWIS: So, to use the formula of Vincent of Lerins, the doctrine of the Real Presence seems to have been universally believed by all Christians at all times and in all places from the beginning, until the Reformation. Even the heretic Berenger of Tours, who denied it around A.D. 1000, was swiftly and clearly labeled a heretic, and I believe he repented. He didn't start a new denomination.

Now if the Real Presence is not true, then for 1500 years God let all of His people believe and practice the idolatry of worshipping bread and wine. As someone put it, how could the Holy Spirit fall asleep on the job for so long? Did all Christians, from the very beginning, fall into any other mistake that was that serious? That seems to me to be a very weighty argument.

GUY: But it's not infallibly true, even if all Christians did believe it, because human beings are not infallible even if they all agree. And even if the Church has always taught it, that doesn't make it infallible if you don't believe what the Roman Catholics believe about the institutional Church being infallible.

LEWIS: But it's still a very, very weighty argument! Authority is not limited to infallibility.

GUY: I disagree with one other thing you said, Jack. I don't think the Eucharist was the *only* serious thing the Church got wrong for a long, long time. There were a lot of other things, like the pope, and prayers to saints, and Mary, and relics, and Purgatory. That's why there had to be a Reformation.

LEWIS: But that doesn't mitigate your difficulty, Guy; it exacerbates it. You have the Holy Spirit letting all the Christians in the world getting not just one thing wrong but a dozen of them from the beginning.

GUY: That's why I believe in *sola scriptura*. Only the Bible is infallible, not the Church.

LEWIS: But the Bible doesn't teach *sola scriptura*, so if you believe only what's in the Bible, you can't believe *sola scriptura*. It's logically self-contradictory. Also, every heretic in history has appealed to the Bible.

GUY: So what? That doesn't prove the Bible isn't infallible.

LEWIS: No, but it proves that we need guidance in interpreting it. That's not a logical proof, but it's a historical proof.

GUY: What do you mean by a historical proof?

LEWIS: Something like this: Take this example. If every country in the world tries to end war by stockpiling weapons for defense, and the result is that every country in the world fights wars, that's a historical proof that stockpiling weapons for defense doesn't work as a way of ending war and ensuring peace.

GUY: I don't get the parallel.

LEWIS: History proves that some things just don't work. You don't abolish war by stockpiling weapons, and you don't abolish heresy by *sola scriptura*.

GUY: Oh. But we're not arguing about how to abolish heresy. There's probably no way to do that. We're arguing about whether we can assume anything except Scripture as infallible. So the only thing that's proved by the fact that every heretic also appeals to Scripture is that *sola scriptura* hasn't, as a historical fact, ended heresies. It doesn't prove that *sola scriptura* is wrong.

LEWIS: That's true. Your argument is logical. (By the way, you never answered my logical argument that *sola scriptura* is logically self-contradictory.) But don't you think that history is a very persuasive practical and probable proof? History is like a laboratory for testing experiments. If every Christian for 1500 years . . .

GUY: You don't find the truth by taking a vote.

LEWIS: No, but when the voting is nearly 100 percent, can you just ignore that consensus?

GRAHAM: Maybe Guy can, but I can't. It bothers me, very seriously, to see the serious disagreements between the different branches of Christendom, especially Protestants versus Catholics. I pray every day for the healing of these wounds in the Body of Christ, though I have no idea how God will do it.

LEWIS: As do I, Billy, as do I. But I think we should return to our focus on the Eucharist and the Real Presence instead of getting into these more general questions of ecumenism, however important they are.

GRAHAM: I agree. So do you have other reasons for your belief in the Real Presence, Jack, besides Tradition?

LEWIS: Yes.

GRAHAM: I'll bet you can guess what my next question is going to be.

LEWIS: What are they, of course. Well, I have a kind of argument from analogy. I see a strong analogy between this issue and four other issues that surround

it, or ground it, or justify it. But it will take a little
time for me to explain it.

GRAHAM: Go ahead, please.

LEWIS: The first issue is religion as such, the religious
world view versus the nonreligious world view. The
religions of the world are obviously very, very different, but they have one thing in common: they all
believe that man is not the highest reality, that there
is something or someone greater than man, and that
consequently the meaning of life is for us to conform
to that, or to Him, to guide our lives by whatever can
be known about this superior reality, whether it's the
God of the Bible or Brahman or Tao or Buddha-mind
or "the will of Heaven", or even just the world of
eternal Platonic Ideas. And all atheists deny that; they
deny that there exists anything, anywhere, superior
to man, and therefore they deny that man's primary
task is to conform his thinking and his living to *that*,
since *that* simply does not exist. So the meaning of
life becomes man's will, man's pleasure, man's power,
man's control of nature. That's a radical difference.
It makes a difference to everything, both in theory
and in practice, in world view and in life-view.

Now one of those two views has to be not only
wrong but disastrously wrong. If the claims of religion—the claims common to all the religions of the
world—are right, then atheists are as wrong as you
can possibly be. They're missing the whole meaning
of life. And if those religious claims are wrong, then
it's the religious believers who are totally and disastrously wrong. They're telling us to guide our whole
lives by a star that isn't there. They're worshipping

a myth, a lie, a hallucination. Freud even goes so far
as to classify all the religions of the world as insanity,
a collective hallucination.

GRAHAM: I follow your reasoning, but I don't see what
it has to do with the Eucharist.

LEWIS: I'm coming to that. Let's look at the next step.
Let's move from the more general to the more specific. The next step is the particular religion that believes that the one true God Himself took the initia-
tive and revealed Himself in history to one specific
people, the Jews; that they, and no one else, are God's
"chosen people", chosen to know the true God; and
they are commanded not to worship any of the thousands of other gods of all the other religions, whether
they have personal names or not.

Christians and Muslims begin there, with Judaism,
and they both accept the Jewish revelation as true,
they accept the God of the Bible as the true God,
and then they both add something else that the Jews
don't: the divinity of Christ for Christianity and the
infallibility of the Koran and Mohammed as the last
and greatest prophet for Islam.

Now this second step, the step to Judaism in particular, the issue of whether to take that step or not
—that is as controversial and as divisive as the first
issue, the truth or falsehood of religion in general.
If the Jews are not what they claim to be, namely,
God's chosen people—chosen for no virtue of their
own, mind you (their own Scriptures make that very
clear), but nevertheless chosen to be God's collective prophet to the world—if this claim isn't true,
then it's the most arrogant claim in the world, and it

explains why anti-Semitism is so common in all the rest of the world. The claim is that the religion of the Jews is not just one of the many human roads up the mountain to God, another yoga or another religious experience, but it's God Himself making the one true road down the mountain. That's why Jews and Christians and Muslims reject that image which almost everybody else believes, that all religious roads are roads that go up the same mountain and meet and agree at the top and that we can see that unity once we reach the top but don't see it as we're climbing up different religious roads. (The claim is implicitly very arrogant, by the way, because it assumes that the claimer is already at the top and can see this unity, while ordinary religious people who are still climbing and see the roads as different are not at the top and can't see that truth.) But this image of many roads up the same mountain can't be true if the claims of Judaism are true because the roads that we make up the mountain to God can't be equal to the road that God Himself made down the mountain to us, any more than man can be equal to God.

So step two is also a radical either/or. You can't stay in the comfortable middle. The Jews are unique: either uniquely privileged and uniquely right or else uniquely arrogant and uniquely wrong. So if you can't reject the Jewish claim, the claim of the Bible, to be divine revelation—if you can't dismiss that as arrogant, egotistic, proud nonsense, then you have to accept it as the unique truth, just as, if you can't dismiss all the religions of the world as a collective hallucination or insanity, then you have to accept their basic radical and life-changing claim. It's an extreme either/or both times.

GRAHAM: I think I see where you're going with this. But go on.

LEWIS: The next step, the next more specific step, is the claim of Christ. He alone among all the great religious founders and teachers and saints and sages and prophets and mystics claims to be the only be-gotten Son of God, the unique God uniquely incarnate in this unique man. If that's true, we all need to fall down at His feet and worship Him; and if that's false, then we need to crucify Him as the world's worst blasphemer and liar, or at least lock him up in a padded cell.

That's the oldest argument in Christian apologet-ics, the "either God or a bad man" argument. It goes back to the early Fathers of the Church. I put it into *Mere Christianity*, and it's been quoted again and again by people who don't know that it's not my original argument at all but very old, very traditional. I think your friend Josh McDowell christened it the "Lord, Liar, or Lunatic" argument. If you can't dismiss Jesus as a liar or a lunatic, then the only alternative is that you simply have to accept Him as the Lord. There's no other possibility. The one thing He can't possibly be is just a good man. A good man who is merely a man and not God, if he is sane and honest, certainly does not claim to be God. If he really believes he's God, then he's a lunatic, in fact the greatest lunatic in the world, And if he knows he isn't God but says he is, then he's a liar, in fact the greatest liar in the world, because that's the biggest lie anyone could possibly tell. It's an absolute either/or again.

GRAHAM: I always thought that was a great argument.

Not just for its logic, but because it forces people to confront His claims honestly; it brings them face to face with Jesus Christ. And I thank you for dusting it off and expressing it so clearly and compellingly for modern man.

LEWIS: Thanks for your thanks. Now here's the last and most specific step in my analogy. In the Eucharist, the Church claims that Christ is really present. And she claims that it's not her invention, but Christ's. He took bread and said that it was His Body, and He took wine and said it was His Blood. And the Church from the beginning has always taken that literally, not just symbolically. If that's not true, then the Church is an idolatrous liar. And so is the Bible, if the Church's uniform interpretation of the Bible for 1500 years is true. If the Real Presence is not true, then what we are really doing in believing that is worshipping bread and wine as if it's God incarnate. It's idolatry. And it's very, very stupid to confuse bread and wine with God because there's an infinite difference between God and these finite material creatures. You see, it's the same either/or. The claim is either a tremendous truth or a tremendous error.

And at every stage, if the claim is true, then the truth about God and what God does is astonishing, not obvious, not a platitude, but a shock. And the fourth claim, the one about the Eucharist, is very close to the third claim, the claim for Christ's divinity, because the Church describes the Eucharist as "the extension of the Incarnation".

So my argument from analogy is that we find the same divine fingerprints on the Eucharist as we find on religion in general, on Judaism, and on Christ. At every stage of divine revelation, we have to choose between extremes, an extreme error or an extreme truth. Either the Eucharist is God incarnate, or it's a mere symbol. Mistaking either one of those two possibilities for the other is a very serious mistake.

TOLKIEN: I see three concrete individuals who typify the same pattern in these three steps from stage one to stage four: Abraham, Saint Paul, and John Henry Newman: from paganism to Judaism, from Judaism to Christianity, and from the Church of England to Catholicism. Each one had to leave all his friends and his spiritual home (and his physical home, too, in the cases of Abraham and Paul) and his previous belief system, which was shattered by God's invitation to move on. You're still on step three, Jack.

LEWIS: We're talking about the Eucharist now, and, on that issue, I'm on step four. The point of my argument is the identical divine fingerprint on all four steps, the same pattern.

GRAHAM: And do you see that "divine fingerprint" on any of the other doctrines in Christianity, or just on the Eucharist?

LEWIS: On many other things, too, because they're parts of the whole Christian claim, parts of Christ's claim. The forgiveness of sins, for instance. When Christ forgave sins, the Jews were scandalized. "Who can forgive sins but God alone?" they argued. And they were right. And the Church inherited that scandalous claim from Him: He said to His Apostles, "If you forgive the sins of any, they are forgiven", and "What you bind on earth shall be bound in Heaven and what you loose on earth shall be loosed in Heaven." He said that to His Apostles, and they continued to exercise that authority down through history when they ordained bishops (or "presbyters") to continue that authority and when those bishops ordained priests to continue that divine forgiveness of sins in the confessional.

GRAHAM: Well, there's the controversy, right? There's the questionable link in the chain, the human link. All Christians agree with what the Bible says Christ said and did, but not all Christians agree with what the Church said and did down through history, including her claiming that her bishops had authority by "apostolic succession" and her doing the things she claims to do in the sacraments like forgiving sins with divine authority.

LEWIS: Of course, it's true that Protestants protest that claim: that's why they're called Protestants. That's my point: my four-step argument from analogy is an argument against that Protestant protest. The protest is against the fourth step in that pattern, that principle. And the protest fits the same pattern as the protest against the other three very controversial claims: for religion in general, for the Jewish God, and for the divinity of Christ. If the Church's claims about the Eucharist are false, and Protestantism is true, then the Catholic Church, the pre-Protestant church, both Roman and Anglican and Eastern Orthodox, is the most arrogant and idolatrous and blasphemous church in the world.

GRAHAM: Well, that's very harsh!

LEWIS: Indeed. That is exactly my point. You can't soften the either/or.

GRAHAM: Oh, but I think we can, and I think we must.

LEWIS: How?

GRAHAM: By what I said before about the heart being more important than the head and that we agree in our hearts' love of the same Lord, even though we disagree about His address.

LEWIS: And I agreed about that. Our hearts are at peace even though our heads are at war. But our hearts' agreement doesn't end our heads' disagreement.

GRAHAM: Perhaps it will in the future. Perhaps the heart will educate the head to see better.

LEWIS: I share your hope, though I don't see how it's possible without compromise, without somehow relativizing or subjectivizing truth. The law of non-contradiction can't be revoked.

GRAHAM: But our understanding can. Perhaps on this issue, Our Lord can help us to understand it aright, if we really ask Him in faith. If we really want to see the truth, how can we do better than to ask Truth Himself to teach us? He promised, "Seek and you shall find", remember.

LEWIS: I don't deny what you say, but that has not happened about any of the other issues that divide us, so I hold very little hope that it can happen on this one, unless this one is very different from the others. But it seems to be of a piece with the others.

GRAHAM: According to your argument.

LEWIS: Yes.

GRAHAM: But perhaps your argument is wrong. It's not part of dogma, is it? Your church hasn't added the works of Lewis to the canon of the Bible yet, has it?

LEWIS: No fear whatsoever of that ever happening, I can guarantee you.

GRAHAM: Who knows? With God all things are possible. Perhaps before the century is finished, Rome and Constantinople will both lift their mutual excommunications from 1054. And perhaps even Luther and the Council of Trent, which excommunicated each other five hundred years later, will reconcile. If hard justice and soft peace can kiss each other when divine truth comes up from the earth and human mercy looks down from Heaven, anything can happen.[1]

LEWIS: That would be a miracle. But God performs miracles.

GRAHAM: So let us keep praying for them.

---

[1] In fact, the two miracles did happen. The mutual excommunications were lifted; and the Vatican and the worldwide council of Lutherans issued the Joint Declaration on Justification, the issue that almost every Evangelical would say was the most important issue of the Reformation, agreeing that the two churches used different language systems to say essentially the same thing concerning justification.

9

Tolkien vs. Lewis

Up to this point, most of the arguing has been between Lewis and Graham, with Tolkien quietly nodding agreement with most of what Lewis said. Now the conversation takes a different turn as Tolkien begins to speak up.

GRAHAM: Tollers, we haven't heard much from you yet. You agree with most of what Jack said, don't you?

TOLKIEN: Most of it, yes, but not all of it. We have some disagreements.

GRAHAM: How important do you think those disagreements are?

TOLKIEN: I can't estimate how important they are, but I can tell you where they are. I think they center on the identity of the Church and on where Christ's authority is to be found. It all depends on how you interpret Henry VIII and his break with Rome and with apostolic succession. The Catholic Church says that Anglican ordinations of bishops and priests are invalid because of that.

GRAHAM: What, exactly, is your theory of apostolic succession?

TOLKIEN: It's not a *theory*, it's a historical fact. Christ told His Apostles to teach with His authority. He said to them, "He who hears you hears Me." And they ordained others to succeed them, and these were called bishops. It's all in the New Testament as well as in secular histories. That's fact, not theory. And those bishops ordained other bishops and priests, claiming to pass on the authority of Christ and the Apostles by that chain of succession, by the sacrament of ordination. That's another historical fact. That's how the authority of Christ gets handed on down through history to us today, just as sexual intercourse is how the biological continuity of the human race gets handed down through history. That's what Sacred Tradition is. We depend on our parents in the faith for our truth about Christ, for our supernatural truth, just as much as we depend on our parents in the flesh for our natural life.

GRAHAM: What about the Bible? That's also a historical fact, and it tells us the historical facts about Christ.

TOLKIEN: Yes, but it, too, had to be handed down through history. The Bible is the written part of Sacred Tradition. But the Bible isn't our immediate link with Christ; the Church is. The Church is also the link between Christ and the Bible. Jesus didn't write the Bible, and He didn't command His Apostles to teach the Bible. He commanded them to teach everything He said and did. He didn't give them a Bible; He gave them a Church. And then, years later, the Church wrote the Bible, the New Testament.

GRAHAM: Those are historical facts, yes, but they don't prove that the Church is as infallible as the Bible.

TOLKIEN: Yes, they do. Because there can't be more in the effect than there is in the cause, so if you deny infallibility in the Church, you have to deny infallibility in the Bible. As so many Protestant churches are doing, becoming modernist or liberal. Which is exactly what you would expect because you deny the middle link in the chain.

GRAHAM: What do you mean?

TOLKIEN: Christ is the first link. The Bible, you say, is your link to Him. But the Church is the connecting link between Christ and the Bible. Once you undo the second link in the chain, you undo the third link, too.

Suppose we change the image. Christ is the magnet, and His authority is like magnetism. Think of four iron rings fastened to the magnet. The first is the Church, which He gave us. The second is the Bible, which the Church gave us. The third is those of us who preach the Bible, like you, and the fourth is the people to whom you preach, the people who come to believe. The magnetism symbolizes truth, authoritative truth, infallible truth, divine truth. It comes to us from Christ, but it comes through the Church first and then the Bible. If you deny either one of those links, the whole chain falls apart.

GRAHAM: But your prophecy isn't coming true. All Protestants deny the infallibility of the Church, but many of us are not becoming modernists and denying the infallibility of the Bible. The chain is not broken for us, at least, though it is for the modernists.

TOLKIEN: Then look at the chain in the other direction, from us up. If we accept what you say, we should accept the Bible. Fine. But if we accept what the Bible says, we should accept the Church, because that's the link between Christ and the Bible and also because the Bible tells us Christ gave us the Church.

GRAHAM: The Bible also is our link to Christ. Truth is truth, whether directly from Christ, which is how the Apostles got it, or through the Church, which is how you get it, or through the Bible, which is how I get it.

TOLKIEN: Well, I guess you can get truth either through a book or through persons, yes. But you can't get sacraments through books. And He told us not just to preach His truths but also to do the sacred work, the public work (that's what "liturgy" means), the sacred rites. That's an essential part of what He told His Apostles to hand on. ("Handing-on" or "handing-down" is the literal meaning of the word "tradition". It's rather like handing on the baton in a relay race.) And that "Sacred Tradition" included not just words but also deeds, which clearly includes sacraments. Read the actual words of what you call "the great commission" in Matthew 28. They could almost be translated: "Be a Catholic."

LEWIS: By the way, He didn't say, "Be a *Roman* Catholic." We Anglicans believe that we still share in what the Creed calls the one, holy, catholic, and apostolic Church and her Tradition and her authority.

TOLKIEN: But the Church that you say you are still a part of, the Catholic Church, says that you *don't*, because Henry the Eighth broke apostolic succession when he broke his union with Rome and started a breakaway church. You call it "the Church of England", but we call it "the Church of Henry" or sometimes "the Church of Henry's Hormones".

LEWIS: Come on, Tollers, you're letting alliteration substitute for accuracy. It wasn't sex, it was sons. It was the succession that Henry demanded. And you guys have even more smelly skeletons in your closet than we have: the Borgia popes, for instance.

TOLKIEN: Indeed, we do. One of our bishops was Judas Iscariot. He was the first Catholic bishop to accept government money. But he was not the last one.

LEWIS: Touché, Tollers. We both harbor criminals in our houses.

GRAHAM: By the time you two get finished, we Protestants will be the last ones standing.

LEWIS: Let's get back to what we're supposed to be talking about now, Tollers: your faith, not mine.

TOLKIEN: Well, part of my faith is that yours is based on a questionable authority. One with six wives and various diseases.

LEWIS: I hate to disenchant your fantasy, Tollers, but we Anglicans haven't yet changed the words of the hymn to read "The Church's one foundation is Henry the Eighth, her lord."

TOLKIEN: Seriously, Jack, don't you ever have any doubts about whether your priests are validly ordained and whether they really have the power to consecrate the Eucharist and bring about the Real Presence and feed us with Christ, not just with bread? And don't you ever doubt whether your sins are really forgiven in the confessional when your breakaway priests say they are? I know how seriously you take that sacrament: you go to confession every week. You know, when Chesterton was asked why he converted from Anglicanism to Catholicism, he replied, "To get my sins forgiven."

LEWIS: As I said a minute ago, I thought we were supposed to be talking about your faith now, not mine. And focusing on the Eucharist.

TOLKIEN: And as I replied a minute ago, we *are* talking about my faith: about what my faith tells me about yours and especially concerning the Eucharist. And my faith tells me these two things: that you are right about what you inherited from us, the theology of the Eucharist, the nature of the Eucharist, about its *essence*—Christ's Real Presence—and that you lack just one little thing: its *existence*!

LEWIS: But we believe you're wrong about that because we don't believe your Church is infallible. We believe we have the Real Presence in our sacraments just as much as you do.

TOLKIEN: But believing you have it doesn't give it to you. Christ alone can give it to you. And He promised it only to His Apostles, who promised it only to their successors, down through the centuries. You broke that chain.

LEWIS: So my issue with your Church is not the theology of the Real Presence—I might even affirm Transubstantiation, if I could understand it and if it did not have the claims of an infallible papacy behind it —but the issue is whether we Anglicans really *have* that Real Presence, whether our bishops and priests have broken apostolic succession.

TOLKIEN: Yes. You have the power if and only if you have the authority. In the Church, might does not make right, but right makes might.

LEWIS: Quite right, Tollers. But I think even you would not deny that Almighty God, who instituted His sacraments, can and does work outside of them.

TOLKIEN: Of course.

LEWIS: And the papal bull that declared Anglican priestly ordinations to be invalid—if I'm not mistaken—that is not an infallible *dogma*, but just an authoritative rule, a precept, a piece of authoritative housekeeping in the Church.

TOLKIEN: "Housekeeping" sounds much too relativistic to me. It's more important than that. It's not a rule about using the mud room to wipe your boots. It's about whether the food your kitchen serves is real food.

LEWIS: But isn't infallibility restricted to dogmas (theological or moral) that can be traced back to the "deposit of faith" given by Christ to the Apostles and to the consensus of the Church Fathers and that have a sign or formula of infallibility attached—either the Vincentian one ("this has been believed by all Christians at all times and places") or the words *ex cathedra*?

TOLKIEN: Yes. And apostolic succession is such a dogma.

LEWIS: Indeed it is, but the application of that dogma to churches that you call schismatic is not.

TOLKIEN: It is authoritative, even if it is not labeled infallible like the dogmas.

LEWIS: And so when your Church applies that dogma of apostolic succession to us Anglicans and says no, you don't have it, and also to the Eastern Orthodox churches, which are also schismatic, and says yes, you do have it, that is authoritative but not infallible. The applications of unchangeable dogma to historically changing things are not dogmas and not infallible. I'm not up on my Roman ecclesiology and canon law and such things, but I think that's right, isn't it?

TOLKIEN: To be perfectly honest with you, I'm not, either. I don't know. But even if it's not infallible, it's clearly authoritative. The authority of the Church is not limited to infallibility or to dogma.

LEWIS: Let's assume I'm wrong and that all Anglican orders are invalid. Does it necessarily follow from that that God does not bring about the Real Presence when a faithful and sincere and saintly Anglican priest believes He does? Is God unable to do that? To work outside His sacraments? You admitted a moment ago that He could.

TOLKIEN: Of course He can, and He does, He gives graces everywhere. But not *sacramental* graces. He instituted sacraments for that.

LEWIS: But isn't it in His style, so to speak, to make exceptions to His own rules?

TOLKIEN: Give me another example.

LEWIS: Chesterton's line about God not obeying His own first commandment, "Thou shalt not make any graven images." He says that God "broke His own law and made a graven image of Himself" when He made mankind in His image. Aren't you being more like the Pharisees than like Christ if you don't give Him that wiggle room?

TOLKIEN: Of course we can't put God in a box. But He instituted special boxes, sacraments, that have an identity that sets them apart. That's what "sacred" *means.* Sacraments are not sacraments unless they are *sacra*, sacred, and there are clear lines defining the sacred. The space outside a church can't be sacred in the same way as the space inside the church. And the time before and after a Mass can't be sacred in the same way as the time in it, the sacred time.

LEWIS: I quite agree. Yet that does not mean that God cannot or would not work "outside the box" and give the power to consecrate the Sacrament to Anglican priests even if we are wrong and you are right about us being schismatic and breaking apostolic succession. Your conclusion does not necessarily follow from your premises.

TOLKIEN: Well, if you are right, then there's no reason to think that God wouldn't bring about the Real

Presence not only for schismatics like Anglicans but even heretics like Protestants who don't even believe in it. He *could* do that, right?

LEWIS: He could do anything that doesn't involve a self-contradiction. But we have good reason to think He wouldn't give the Real Presence to those who don't believe in it and aren't open to it, as we Anglicans are.

Look, Tollers, here's my bottom line: If the papal bull that declared Anglican orders invalid isn't infallible, then it might be wrong.

TOLKIEN: And here's my bottom line: Even if I'm not certain that you don't have valid orders and the Real Presence, you can't be certain that you do! It's possible, but you need more than possibility, you need certainty. This is not just a matter of theory and theology; it is one of practice and religion. It's not just thinking, it's eating. You need to know it's real food you're eating. You need to know that that is Christ's real Body and Blood that you adore and receive. Your faith can't be in a possibility!

LEWIS: Tollers, I want to direct your attention to something you have ignored.

TOLKIEN: What's that?

LEWIS: The expression on Guy's face. Look how much he's enjoying every moment of this squabble between us. That devilish grin is why I never discuss our internecine battles in public or in print. It feeds into the Enemy's strategy of "divide and conquer."

TOLKIEN: But we're just four friends here. Nobody is taking down this debate. Nobody will publish it.

LEWIS: You never know.

TOLKIEN: What, do you think there is some invisible fly on the wall?

LEWIS: Who knows? He may be some twenty-first-century author who took a time machine into the past and who is writing all this down to send to a publisher to print and sell long after we die. Some traitor, some intellectual prostitute who peddles his mind for filthy lucre. He's probably an American.

TOLKIEN: Seriously, Jack, I'm sorry if I've upset you by becoming personal in my jibes. I know you're allergic to my bringing up that issue between us, for the sake of our friendship. But that issue has got to be very seriously disconcerting to you, not just mentally but personally; you can't be sure that your sins are really forgiven when your priests pronounce forgiveness.

LEWIS: I can be sure God forgives me. He promised it.

TOLKIEN: In the Bible.

LEWIS: Yes.

TOLKIEN: Now you sound more like a Protestant than a Catholic.

LEWIS: Well, let it be so then. Perhaps on that issue I am.

TOLKIEN: And you can't be sure that you're receiving Christ's actual Body and Blood when you receive the Eucharist as consecrated by your priests if they have broken apostolic succession. Christ didn't give that power to everyone who claims it. And that's not just a theological dispute; that's like the difference between getting real food or only pretend food when you eat. A rather large difference, if you need that food to live.

LEWIS: Even if you are right about that—which I am convinced you are not—I know I have His life in me. I know the two most important things in the world: I know who I am, and I know who He is. I am His saved, and He is my Savior.

TOLKIEN: You know that by faith.

LEWIS: Yes, by faith.

TOLKIEN: Again, you sound like a Protestant.

LEWIS: Again, I accept the label. But I also accept the label of Catholic. And I do *not* accept the divisions between us and the mutual excommunications between us that have darkened our history and that are now darkening our conversation.

TOLKIEN: Nor do I. But there is only one way to end them.

LEWIS: And what is that?

TOLKIEN: Come home, O prodigal son.

LEWIS: I cannot.

TOLKIEN: You can.

LEWIS: Well, then, I will not. I choose to stay with this fine ship. It is not a pigsty.

TOLKIEN: Like Noah's ark, you mean. You prefer a spiffy new little English yacht to the old pigsty of the Ark. Well, I choose His boat over yours.

LEWIS: You have refuted my pigsty analogy but not my argument.

TOLKIEN: What argument? I didn't hear an argument.

GUY: You two are really getting into it now, Oxford-style! This is fun.

TOLKIEN: To the devil, it certainly is. Seriously, Jack, I'd like to know just what is stopping you from going all the way? You moved from atheism to theism, from theism to mere Christianity, and from mere Christianity to Anglicanism. What's keeping you away from the last step, coming home to Rome?

LEWIS: Like the prodigal son.

TOLKIEN: Exactly.

LEWIS: I'll tell you what is stopping me, if you insist. In terms of the parable of the prodigal son, what is stopping me is the attitude of my older brother, whom I had thought was my closest friend but who is now acting like my judge and jury.

TOLKIEN: I'm sorry, Jack. Now it's my turn to say touché to you. Certainly, our friendship should not depend on our theological agreement.

10

Tolkien's Faith
and Graham's Critique

LEWIS: Can we get back to comparing theologies now? We've agreed to be friends; that's easy. What's hard is to agree in theology. Is there a possible reconciliation between us there?

GRAHAM: Thanks for getting us back on track, Jack. Let me suggest one possible reconciliation. Tollers, even if you are right about your theology of the sacraments and about apostolic succession and about the Anglicans not having it, don't you think God would give to a holy and faith-filled Anglican Christian like Jack here as much grace when he partook of his sacraments as He would give to a Roman Catholic?

TOLKIEN: No, I don't.

GRAHAM: Why not?

TOLKIEN: Because that would be to say it didn't make a real difference whether you have the authority of Christ or not. That would be like Christ commanding us to do it His way, and when we instead did it our way, He rewarded us anyway, exactly as if the difference between His way and our way really made no difference at all.

GRAHAM: Don't you believe that, all other things being equal, the more faith you have, the more grace you get? The more you open your mouth, the more food can come in.

TOLKIEN: Yes, that's right.

GRAHAM: So it all depends on faith.

TOLKIEN: No, I don't think it *all* depends on faith.. Because you need *two* things to happen if you are going to be nourished by food. You need to open your mouth in faith, yes, but the food also needs to be real! So whether Christ is really, objectively present in the Communion wafer that I eat has to make a difference.

GRAHAM: Well, then, I think we're back to my difficulty about your view of the sacraments being magical. I don't find that kind of *ex opere operato* magic in the Gospels.

TOLKIEN: I do.

GRAHAM: Where?

TOLKIEN: In many places. For instance, if the woman with the lifelong hemorrhage had touched the hem of Saint Peter's garment in the crowd instead of Christ's, she would *not* have been miraculously healed, even if she had had deep faith and very good intentions.

GRAHAM: Well we don't know what would have happened, do we?

TOLKIEN: I think we do. Christ Himself said He felt power go out from Himself when she touched Him. Saint Peter does not have that power. No one can work miracles but God.

GRAHAM: Is God bound by only one method in working miracles?

TOLKIEN: No, He is not.

GRAHAM: Then we do not know what would have happened if she had touched the wrong garment.

TOLKIEN: I grant you that. But we do know that Christ makes a real difference.

GRAHAM: Indeed we do. But we don't know how He administers that difference, that power, that grace. Even if you're right about the sacraments, about them being real channels of real grace, you don't know that there are no other channels or how much grace He gives through those other channels, especially through pure faith, simple faith, faith alone.

TOLKIEN: It's true that I don't know that. But it's also true that I know that He instituted the sacraments to give grace. We don't have any dogmas about the non-existence of grace outside the sacraments, but we do have a dogma about its existence in the sacraments.

In fact, Christ Himself is the primary sacrament. If He had never become incarnate and died on the Cross and given us His Body and Blood on the Cross, that certainly would have made all the difference in the world, right?

GRAHAM: Of course.

TOLKIEN: Then we could not be saved, right?

GRAHAM: Right. The Bible tells us that: "Without the shedding of blood, there is no remission of sins."

TOLKIEN: Even if we had faith?

GRAHAM [after a hesitation]: Yes . . . I think so. Our faith has an object, and that object is Christ, not itself.

TOLKIEN: Then faith alone does not save us.

GRAHAM: Of course not; only Christ can save us. I still say that faith alone is all we need subjectively. We also need Christ objectively. Christ is our food, and faith opens our mouth.

TOLKIEN: You just summarized Catholic Eucharistic theology very nicely.

GRAHAM: I meant it symbolically. Faith opens the mouth of our spirit.

TOLKIEN: And we Catholics mean it literally, as we believe that Christ meant both "This is My Body" and "take and eat this" literally.

GRAHAM: Well, we Protestants don't.

TOLKIEN: But that's bad literary criticism!

GRAHAM: What in the world do you mean?

TOLKIEN: Look at the context. You know your Bible, Billy. You have to be a good literary critic when you read the Bible, because even though it's a divine book, it's a human book, too—it's got a human nature as well as a divine nature, like Christ. And you know

that one of the basic principles of literary criticism is
to interpret every sentence in its context. So let's look
at the context of the words of Christ when He instituted the Eucharist at the Last Supper. He's not out in
the wilderness now; He's at table celebrating Passover
and giving the Twelve literal bread and literal wine,
at table, and He's doing this, not casually, but seriously, ceremonially. He's instituting a new Passover.
He calls it a "new covenant", and you know how serious and central the covenant is for the Jews. It's their
umbilical cord to God. And He's instituting this new
thing for all time, just before He is going to die, as
His way of being present with them forever. So now,
in this context, watch how carefully He chooses His
words. He doesn't say, "Take and eat this, but I don't
mean that literally. This bread is only a symbol of
My Body, and your eating it is only a symbol of your
faith." That's a really strained literary interpretation.
It's like interpreting the words of a ship's captain to
his sailors when his ship is sinking and he says, "grab
onto this life preserver with your hands", as meaning
"Don't take me literally; what I mean by your hands
is your faith, and what I mean by the life preserver
is my love."

GRAHAM: I guess we will just have to agree to disagree about interpreting His words.

TOLKIEN: One of us is making a very serious mistake.

GRAHAM: Yes, we both admitted that.

TOLKIEN: But don't you think that Our Lord, with
His divine intelligence, would have foreseen that all of
His followers, every Christian in the world, would be

making that very serious mistake for 1500 years, and wouldn't He have cautioned them against it? Was He ignorant of the fact that He was instituting a sacrament that all His followers would idolize and that His one holy catholic and apostolic Church would officially teach that idolatry?

GRAHAM: I don't know the answer to those questions with certainty. But neither do you.

TOLKIEN: But isn't it very reasonable?

GRAHAM: I still do not agree with your theology, but I do agree that it sounds more reasonable than I thought before.

TOLKIEN: More biblical, too, I hope.

GRAHAM: Perhaps. But what do you believe about the other sacraments? We find only two in the New Testament, Baptism and the Lord's Supper, and you add five more and make it seven.

TOLKIEN: We find the other five in the New Testament, too, though not as clearly.

GRAHAM: And your Church didn't define the definitive list—these seven, no more, no less—until centuries later.

TOLKIEN: That's true. But the Church also didn't definitively define the canon, the list of the books that are divine revelation, the twenty-seven books of the New Testament, until a few centuries later, either. How else do you know that these four Gospels are true and the other ones false, like the Gospel of Thomas or the Gospel of Judas? Only by the Church, not by the Bible. The Bible doesn't include a table of contents.

GRAHAM: By universal use. Those twenty-seven books were always treated as divine revelation.

TOLKIEN: Yes, used by the Church, treated as revelation by the Church.

GRAHAM: We have no objection to the authority of the Church when she defines the Bible. We have objections to the Church when she defines new things, new dogmas.

TOLKIEN: But she doesn't do that. She doesn't define new things; she defines old things, when they're denied by new heresies. Her dogmas are the things that she has always believed.

GRAHAM: Like prayers to saints and the veneration of Mary, and relics, and Purgatory?

TOLKIEN: Yes. They go back to the beginning.

GRAHAM: The record is far from clear about them.

TOLKIEN: But there is no record of controversies about them. They were never denied. If they were new inventions, as you claim, there certainly would have been some dissension about them, some controversy. Where are all the early Protestants? The only ones we have any record of are the heretics, like the Iconoclasts, who did deny one of the things you usually deny, the rightness of images and statues. And they were clearly labeled heretics.

GRAHAM: Frankly, I don't know enough of the details about Church history to refute you there . . .

TOLKIEN: That's why you're a Protestant.

GRAHAM [ignoring the insult]: Let's get back to the sacraments, if you please. Do you believe that all seven of your sacraments give grace in the same way?

TOLKIEN: That depends on what you mean by "the same way". In one sense, no, because only the Eucharist is Christ Himself, His very Body and Blood, and thus something to be rightly adored and worshipped. But they all give grace. In fact, Baptism gives first grace, saving grace, eternal life; but we don't worship the water in Baptism because it's just water, not Christ, though it's used by Christ.

That's why He was baptized in the Jordan even though He had no sins to wash away: the water didn't cleanse Him; He cleansed the water and gave it the power to be His instrument to cleanse us in Baptism.

All the sacraments give grace but in different ways. But, in one sense, they all give grace in the same way in that they all work *ex opere operato*, objectively and not just subjectively, and through some material means.

GRAHAM: But you also believe that the subjective dimension counts, too, don't you? That how much grace you get depends on how open and faithful and holy your soul is.

TOLKIEN: Yes. I've admitted that twice already.

GRAHAM: And that when the New Testament talks about faith, it doesn't mean just intellectual belief, because "the devils also believe, but tremble with fear."

TOLKIEN: Right.

GRAHAM: So we agree on the subjective dimension, at least. You need faith in the personal sense, not just the intellectual sense, to be saved.

TOLKIEN: Yes, but we Catholics say it's not by "faith alone", but by faith and good works, the works of love. James says that very explicitly.

GRAHAM: What he means is that good works are the expression of saving faith. Love and the works of love are the natural and necessary fruit of faith, as figs are the fruit of a fig tree. The visible proof of the invisible reality.

TOLKIEN: They're two parts of the same thing, as the figs and the roots are two parts of the same fig tree.

GRAHAM: I agree with that. It's the same Christ, and the same Holy Spirit of Christ, that comes into us by faith and, through us, into the world by the works of love. I think we essentially agree about faith and works, because we accept the same data, the biblical data. And even though we don't agree about *ex opere operato* in the sacraments, we agree that it's only Christ who is the ultimate object of our faith. Even if you speak of seven sacraments, you don't speak of seven saviors.

TOLKIEN: True. But what we disagree about is how He does it, about how the Savior saves, about whether He does it through objective sacraments or not. We agree that He saves us through faith, but we don't agree that He saves us through "faith alone".

LEWIS: To clarify, Protestants say faith is sufficient as well as necessary, and Catholics say it is necessary but not sufficient.

GRAHAM: And we both agree that Christ instituted at least two sacraments, but we don't agree that they work *ex opere operato*.

TOLKIEN: Oh, I think we do, at least for Baptism—all except Baptists, who don't accept infant Baptism.

GRAHAM: What in the world do you mean? That's a Roman Catholic formula. Protestants don't accept that.

TOLKIEN: Oh, I know you don't like the formula. But a rose by any other name would not only smell as sweet but would still be a rose. But perhaps I am wrong about that. *You* must tell me what you believe; I can't tell you. So please tell me if I'm wrong here. I think most of you Protestants believe we get grace in the two sacraments in which you do believe, namely, Baptism and the Lord's Supper, don't you, even though you don't believe it comes through the objective matter of the sacrament but only through your subjective, personal faith—isn't that right?

GRAHAM: Yes.

TOLKIEN: And if you baptize infants, then that grace has got to work *ex opere operato*, or objectively, because an infant can't have any personal, subjective faith yet at all.

GRAHAM: That's precisely why most Baptists don't believe in infant Baptism.

TOLKIEN: But what about the majority of Protestants, who do? How do they explain where faith fits in infant Baptism?

GRAHAM: They believe that it's our faith that is the power, so to speak, the power to open our hearts and accept God's grace. It's not the material sacrament itself.

TOLKIEN: But whose faith? An infant can't have faith yet.

GRAHAM: The parents' faith.

TOLKIEN: Because the parents are part of the Church, Christ's people.

GRAHAM: Yes.

TOLKIEN: So it's the faith of the Church. But why isn't it the sacraments of the Church?

GRAHAM: Because it's faith alone, not Baptism, that saves you. Baptism is a good work, but good works don't save you. All Protestants believe that, whether they're Baptists or not.

TOLKIEN: I see. So the dispute between the Baptists and other Protestants about infant Baptism is not the main thing. Both Protestant "sides", so to speak, agree that it's faith alone that saves you.

GRAHAM: Yes. It's faith alone that saves you, but faith does not remain alone; it motivates good works.

TOLKIEN: But the good works do not save you. And Baptism is a good work. So Baptism does not save you.

GRAHAM: That logically follows.

TOLKIEN: But the Bible explicitly contradicts that. There's a verse in 1 Peter that says "Baptism . . . saves you." What do you do with that?

GRAHAM: We say it means that Baptism saves you only as an expression of faith; just as your witness, your words, your public profession of faith saves you, not by some kind of magic in the words, but only because those words express your faith.

TOLKIEN: Faith is a matter of individual free choice, isn't it? I can't be saved by your faith, only by my own faith, right?

GRAHAM: Right.

TOLKIEN: Let's put these things together. Point One: The Bible says that Baptism saves you. Point Two: You say that salvation is by faith alone. Point Three: An infant can't yet have faith. Point Four: We can't have another person's faith. All four of those points can't be true. There's a logical inconsistency there somewhere. And I think you avoid it by denying the one point the Bible explicitly teaches, word for word, that Baptism saves you. Peter says that. I avoid it by denying the one thing that the Bible also explicitly contradicts, again word for word, namely, that we are saved, or justified, by faith alone. James says that. So which of us is adding to the Bible, and which is going by what the Bible says?

GRAHAM: Hmmm. Let me start with something simple and concrete. Baptism is a kind of consecration to God, like Mary and Joseph presenting the infant Jesus at the Temple. So the parents' present faith includes a hope that their child will have his own personal faith in the future. Hope is faith directed to the future.

TOLKIEN: So it's like a prophecy. They are prophesying a future faith in their child.

GRAHAM: No, I wouldn't call it prophecy, because all authentic prophecies, all prophecies that are inspired by God, infallibly come true; but there's no guarantee that this child will be a believer. That would make the sacrament like magic and an automatic machine.

TOLKIEN: Then where is the faith?

GRAHAM: In two places, I think: it's a certain faith that they have in the Christ who commanded Baptism, and it's an uncertain faith and an uncertain hope that their child will profess his own personal faith when he's older.

TOLKIEN: So the hoped-for future in some way determines the present? Causality works backwards?

GRAHAM: I think it's something like the Jews of Old Testament times: they were saved by faith in the Christ to come, the Messiah. Frankly, I don't know how it "works". But I do know that we're saved by grace alone, through faith alone, not by grace plus anything else, like sacraments or good works.

TOLKIEN: You say you "know" that. You mean you *believe* that, don't you?

GRAHAM: Yes. But faith is a kind of knowledge. It tells you the truth.

TOLKIEN: That's true of *the* Faith, the Christian faith, divine revelation. But it's not necessarily true of *your* faith.

GRAHAM: Why not?

TOLKIEN: Because different Christians believe different things, mutually contradictory things, and contradictions can't both be objectively true, even though they can both be subjectively believed.

GRAHAM: That's true.

TOLKIEN: So you believe that faith alone saves you, not Baptism.

GRAHAM: Yes.

TOLKIEN: Exactly *why* do you believe that?

GRAHAM: That's what the Bible teaches.

TOLKIEN: But it doesn't. We've just seen that it teaches exactly the opposite.

GRAHAM: Well, that's a matter of interpretation.

TOLKIEN: No, it's literal and explicit, in so many words, and as clear as it possibly could be in that passage in 1 Peter. It says that "Baptism saves you."

GRAHAM: We're going round and round about this. We Protestants differ among ourselves as to just what happens in Baptism. Some actually believe in "baptismal regeneration". But that's not the essential thing, I think.

TOLKIEN: What? Regeneration is not the essential thing? Eternal life is not the essential thing?

GRAHAM: No, of course it is. I meant that the essential thing for us to do is not to understand it but to do it, to obey Christ's command to baptize. As with the Eucharist, where He didn't say, "Take and understand this", but "Take and eat this", so with Baptism He didn't say, "Understand this", but "Do this." A philosopher like Socrates would have said: "Understand this", or "Prove this", but Jesus wasn't a philosopher.

TOLKIEN: But that's exactly my point: since He wasn't a philosopher, He didn't say, "This is My Mind", He said "This is My Body." And He said that if you eat of His Body you get eternal life!

GRAHAM: I know He said that, but I believe He meant His Body that would die on the Cross and resurrect. And we "eat" it by faith. And even when we literally eat the bread in the Lord's Supper, that's a symbol, which we understand through faith, of His Body that died on the Cross for our sins. That's the Body that saves us, not the Eucharist, which is only a symbol of that.

TOLKIEN: But when He said those words ("This is My Body"), He was not talking about the Cross, which was future and which would happen the next day, He was talking about the Eucharist, which was present. In fact, He was creating the Eucharist, or inventing the Eucharist, at that very moment! You have to interpret a passage in its context, remember. He took bread and said, essentially, "*This* is My Body. It will be given up for you tomorrow on the Cross. But it is here, present, not future, and presented to you as a present, a gift, in this present moment. You must eat it. Not tomorrow, but now." Notice the unity of the three meanings of "present"—present in time, present in space, and presented as a present, a gift. And He took wine and said, "*This* is My Blood. You must drink it." He didn't point to His veins when He said, "This is My Blood." They already knew that. What was new was that this thing, this thing outside His veins, this thing that looks like wine, this is now His Blood. He didn't say, "When I die on the Cross, *that* will be what you have to eat and drink, by your faith in it. That's what I mean by eating and drinking: not what you are about to do now, with your mouths, but what you will do then, with your mind and heart, with your soul. It is only a metaphor— a new and strange one, one that no Jew ever used —for believing. I am inventing a new metaphor for faith." That is a very strained interpretation. And isn't it strange that that highly symbolic interpretation of yours is present, not among us Catholics, who have always interpreted Scripture on multiple levels, both literal and symbolic, but among you Protestants, especially those who tend to a fundamentalist and literalist theory of interpreting Scripture. You try to interpret everything in Scripture literally—except when it speaks of the Eucharist!

GRAHAM: I'm sorry, your literal interpretation may make sense in terms of your literary criticism, but not in terms of the big picture of biblical theology.

TOLKIEN: It still sounds too much like pagan magic and materialism for you.

GRAHAM: Yes.

TOLKIEN: Interpreting "eat My Body and drink My Blood" literally is a theology appropriate for cannibals.

GRAHAM: Yes.

TOLKIEN: That was exactly the argument the pagan enemies of Christianity used in the first few centuries! And none of the Church Fathers replied to that argument that it was only symbolic, not literal!

GRAHAM: Well, perhaps the critics were close to the truth. Your Catholic theology of the Eucharist seems to me too close to a theology for animals.

TOLKIEN: And your "faith alone" theology sounds too much like a theology for angels.

GRAHAM: It's more spiritual than yours.

TOLKIEN: Yes. It is more spiritual. That's the whole problem. It's the old Gnosticism, which was the father of nearly all the heresies in history.

GRAHAM: I reject both of those heresies, pagan materialism and Gnostic spiritualism. I agree that we are saved, not just by thought, but by His bodily death and Resurrection. That's the object of our faith, not just His mind or His teachings. I agree with you there. What separates us is not spiritualism versus materialism. I'm not a spiritualist, and you're not a materialist. What separates us is not Jesus or the Cross, thank God. But what separates us is the Eucharist. I believe the Bible clearly teaches that it's His death on the Cross that saves us, not a sacrament. That's the Body that saves us.

TOLKIEN: Indeed it is. But how do we get it?

GRAHAM: By faith.

TOLKIEN: By faith alone?

GRAHAM: Yes, by faith alone.

TOLKIEN: No, you can receive a mind by faith alone, you can receive an idea by faith alone, you can adopt a belief by faith alone. But you can't receive a body by faith alone. You receive a body in a bodily way. You get fed the body of a dead cow in a hamburger, not in a belief.

GRAHAM: But even that requires some faith: faith that the hamburger is edible, real meat.

TOLKIEN: You're right. You need faith, too. You need that faith to motivate you to eat it. But you also need actually to eat it. The New Testament always puts those two things together, matter and spirit. It always connects faith and Baptism, for instance in the verse in John 3 where Jesus says to Nicodemus "Unless you are born again *of water* and of the Spirit you cannot enter the Kingdom of Heaven." You need both, because we are both, and God designed our religion for both, for bodies and souls, not for mere bodies, like animals, or mere spirits, like angels. Just as the merely material reception of the sacraments without faith is not enough (they're not magic), so the merely spiritual belief alone is not enough, either.

GRAHAM: I thought you and Jack both admitted that faith alone *was* enough to save you—the Good Thief, for instance, was saved without time for sacraments or good works.

TOLKIEN: You're right. But he was the exception.

GRAHAM: So he got in—without using the front door, the sacramental way.

TOLKIEN: Something like that, yes.

GRAHAM: So you don't think I'm unsaved, then, because I've never received your Catholic sacraments?

TOLKIEN: Not at all.

GRAHAM: Why not?

TOLKIEN: Because as we both admitted, God can work outside His sacraments if He wants to. He can provide back doors into Heaven even though He set up the Church and her sacraments as the front door. Also because you *did* receive the first and most necessary sacrament, Baptism. And Protestant Baptisms are valid, unless they're deliberately intended to be NOT Catholic Baptisms.

GRAHAM: But I've never received any other valid sacrament, according to your theology. And according to your Church, even my Baptism may be invalid if the preacher deliberately intended it contrary to what the Church teaches. That's why she rebaptizes converts conditionally, with the formula "If you have not been baptized, I baptize you . . ." Isn't that true?

TOLKIEN: Yes . . .

GRAHAM: Then do you worry that I might not be saved because I lack your Church and your sacraments? Do you worry that I might go to Hell instead of Heaven?

TOLKIEN: No.

GRAHAM: Why not?

TOLKIEN: First, because that's none of my business. It's God's business. When Jesus' disciples asked him whether many would be saved, He said simply, "Strive to enter in." In other words, "Mind your own business." Not because it's not important but because it's far too important: we have to be sure we're on the right road ourselves first, so that we're not the blind leading the blind. And as for the other person, God only knows, we don't, and we shouldn't claim to know.

GRAHAM: But if you had to bet on it, you'd bet on my salvation, I hope.

TOLKIEN: Of course I would.

GRAHAM: Why?

TOLKIEN: Because I think you deserve to say the words the great martyr Saint Thomas More said when the King's archbishop tried to instill doubt in his mind on the steps of the chopping block. More said, "I go to God", and the archbishop asked him, "Are you quite sure of that, Thomas?" And Thomas replied, calmly, "He will not turn away one who is so blithe to see Him."

GRAHAM: So if you mean by "one who is so blithe to see Him" "one who has such faith in Him", then you are saying that faith alone *can* save you.

TOLKIEN: Yes, I do believe that, as I said. But I believe that only because I believe in what the Church says and not only what the Bible says. Because the Bible says you need faith *and Baptism*, and that seems to leave you out if you were not validly baptized; but the Church has interpreted that to include what it calls "the baptism of desire". If you have just decided to have faith in Christ and you are killed by a runaway truck as you cross the street on your way to the church to receive Baptism, you are not going to Hell because of one drunk truck driver. God can work outside of His sacraments, too.

GRAHAM: I am relieved to hear you say that. So your Church doesn't teach that all Protestants are headed for Hell.

TOLKIEN: Certainly not.

GRAHAM: They, too, can get to Heaven, not by the Catholic front door, but by the Protestant back door. (The front door being faith and Baptism, and the back door being faith alone.)

TOLKIEN: Something like that, yes.

GRAHAM: Then there must be a pretty big crowd entering His house by the back door.

TOLKIEN: No one knows the population statistics, but that would not at all surprise me.

GRAHAM: It delights me to hear you say that.

TOLKIEN: God is very, very gracious.

GRAHAM: Clearly, we both know the same God.

TOLKIEN: Ours is not a different *theos*, but it *is* a different *logos*, a different theology.

GRAHAM: Well . . . yes. But not so very, very different, I hope.

TOLKIEN: And ours is the same Christ, but different churches.

GRAHAM: That's the real question, I think: churches. I don't mean the historical question here, I mean the personal question. Tell me, Tollers, if you don't mind my getting personal: I just don't understand why you feel the need to add the Church and the sacraments to Jesus. Jesus is enough for me. Isn't He enough for you?

TOLKIEN: He is.

GRAHAM: Then you must be a Catholic because you want something *in addition* to Him.

TOLKIEN: No, I'm a Catholic because I want all of Him, more of Him, including all the things He gave us, which include a Church and sacraments. They're not additions to Him; they ARE Him. The Church is His Body. And so is the Host in the Sacrament.

GRAHAM: But it's the same Christ only a different sacramental theology. We Protestants say the sacraments are symbols of Christ, and you Catholics say they are Christ, or contain Christ, or that Christ performs the miracle of a substantial change in them.

TOLKIEN: Yes. Our difference about Baptism is whether it makes a substantial change in the soul, from natural life to supernatural life, from Adam to Christ, from Original Sin to salvation from sin. And our difference about the Eucharist is whether it makes a substantial change from bread and wine to Christ's Body and Blood.

GRAHAM: So our difference about Baptism is the same as our difference about the Eucharist: in both sacraments you believe there is a substantial change, and we don't.

TOLKIEN: Yes. For us, it's substance; for you, it's just symbol.

GRAHAM: And the essential reason why you believe that is the authority of the Church. You extend infallibility to the Church, not just the Bible.

TOLKIEN: No, it's more historically accurate to say that we did not extend infallibility; you shrunk it to *sola scriptura*. We came first. We didn't break off from you; you broke off from us.

GRAHAM: We tried to reform you, but you wouldn't listen.

TOLKIEN: That wasn't just a Reformation, that was a revolution. The Church did need a reformation, and she got it, in the Council of Trent, but she didn't need a revolution. A reformation stays within; a revolution is a rebellion, a war.

GRAHAM: I know that is the key historical issue between us. But I still think that we are more united than divided even here; that we are essentially "on the same page", as we Americans say; and I do accept you as a brother in Christ.

TOLKIEN: So you're not worried about my salvation?

GRAHAM: No.

TOLKIEN: But, after all, if you're right, I'm an idolater.

GRAHAM: I no more think you are going to Hell than you think I am. I think we both trust the same Christ for our salvation.

TOLKIEN: But that has not solved our divisions. Do you think they can ever be resolved?

GRAHAM: I certainly hope so. Our Lord wants it. He prayed passionately for it in John 17. And Paul is constantly calling for unity, for right belief, for orthodoxy.

TOLKIEN: But how? The only way I can see it is for you Protestants to come home.

GRAHAM: And the only way I can see it is for you Catholics to accept our demands for biblical reform.

TOLKIEN: Perhaps there is a third way. Perhaps, as our Eastern Orthodox brethren love to say, orthopraxy can teach orthodoxy—right practice can teach right belief. If we all became saints, I think we would be surprised at how our minds came together once our hearts came together.

GRAHAM: I long for that day when we can stand together and kneel together and worship together and serve our common Lord and Savior together. Perhaps the way of orthopraxy is the only way; perhaps only if we *do* it together, that will help us to *understand* it together.

TOLKIEN: I agree that that would be wonderful, but how? What do you see as the way to this Utopian dream?

GRAHAM: Well, we could begin with intercommunion. We Protestants invite you Catholics to participate in our Eucharist; why do you Catholics forbid us Protestants to participate in yours?

TOLKIEN: We don't forbid you to worship with us, in fact, we invite you, up to the point of receiving the consecrated Host. Come to Mass, by all means, and worship with us. But we can't invite you Protestants to receive the consecrated Host because you don't believe it is anything more than ordinary bread, so that would be a sacrilege, an offense against something sacred, and that would be inviting you to do something that is objectively wrong, wrong in itself, even if you had the best of personal intentions, and we don't want to invite you to do anything wrong.

GRAHAM: I understand, I think. But I don't like it.

TOLKIEN: Neither do I. But at least you understand our motives.

GRAHAM: Yes.

TOLKIEN: Are you optimistic, Billy? Do you think it's even possible to unite without compromise and without one of the two sides simply saying it's wrong? Truth is an absolute, after all, just as much as love is.

GRAHAM: We can't see how that's possible, can we? But that doesn't mean God can't see that. And it doesn't mean God can't do that. "With God all things are possible."

TOLKIEN: So you do have hope.

GRAHAM: Yes. More than you do, I think.

TOLKIEN: That's because you are an optimist.

GRAHAM: No, that's because I believe the Bible.

TOLKIEN: Where does the Bible say anything about that?

GRAHAM: Well, the Bible tells me that when Christ comes again He will marry His Church. And Christ is not a bigamist. He does not marry a harem, but only a single Bride.

TOLKIEN: You are more "ecumenical" than most other Evangelicals are, I think.

GRAHAM: I would not say all that I have said to you publicly, or to most of my Protestant friends, but I think honesty compels me to say it to you. I share your passion for unity, though not your Catholic road to it.

TOLKIEN: Thank you for being so candid, Billy. I wish I could be as optimistic as you are.

GRAHAM: It's not optimism; it's hope. Optimism rests on us; hope rests on God.

TOLKIEN: Good point! And I know it's foolish of me to let my own weak faith and pitiful imagination put limits on what God can do—the God for whom all things are possible. But I'm still pretty skeptical of the optimism of most of the people who are in the forefront of this "ecumenical movement". They seem to love unity more than they love truth.

GRAHAM: Is that true of any one of the four of us? Have any one of us compromised what he believes to be the truth one tiny little bit today in this little bit of ecumenical dialogue?

TOLKIEN: Absolutely not!

GRAHAM: And have we made no progress toward understanding each other? Not one tiny little bit of progress?

TOLKIEN: Of course we have.

GRAHAM: Without compromising truth.

TOLKIEN: Yes.

GRAHAM: Have we come a little closer together than we were a few hours ago?

TOLKIEN: We have.

GRAHAM: And it was mutual, not just one-sided, wasn't it?

TOLKIEN: I think so.

GRAHAM: So I think you've moved closer to me as well as I to you, even though we're both pretty stubborn mules. And without compromising our convictions.

TOLKIEN: We've come closer in feelings anyway, in brotherhood, if not in theology.

GRAHAM: Oh, Tollers, please don't reduce brotherhood to a feeling!

TOLKIEN: I stand corrected. So it's more than a feeling but less than a theological conversion. What is it?

GRAHAM: Hmmm . . . I believe it's called Christian love.

LEWIS: You're learning to use our British irony, Billy!

TOLKIEN: It's not just love, it's understanding, too. I think even though we're no closer to agreement, we understand each other better than we did before.

GRAHAM: We do, and that's *because* of our love for each other in Christ. Love opens our minds as well as our hearts. Orthopraxy leading orthodoxy. We're on that road.

LEWIS: And isn't it remarkable that that closeness came about precisely through discussing our *farness*, our differences, rather than by ignoring them?

11

Tolkien's Deeper Faith
and Graham's Deeper Critique

GRAHAM: Gentlemen, I'd like to push this enterprise one more step, with your permission. I'd like to hear one more thing from you. Tollers, before we finish (and it is getting late): I'd like to hear what the Eucharist means to you, not just theologically, but personally. I didn't come here to debate and argue, though I freely entered into the argument, and I enjoyed it. But I came here to meet you—both of you —and to listen to you and to try to understand "what makes you tick".

TOLKIEN: That's another Americanism, isn't it?

GRAHAM: Yes. I fear we are so enamored of our technology that we subconsciously see people as clocks! And I fear I am guilty of a kind of clock-idolatry myself: I usually obey my schedule, which is busy and full and rigid with obligations. I forget Our Lord's liberating words about time: that the Sabbath was made for man, not man for the Sabbath. Clock time and schedules are made for man, and man is made for God, and I fear our whole culture, especially in

America, usually gets that upside down and backwards. We want God to serve us, and we serve our timetables. Well, I won't do that now. Guy, what is on our schedule for tomorrow morning?

GUY: Well, you rise at six and pray for an hour and grab a quick breakfast, and then we have three staff meetings during the morning, before your public appearance after lunch. If we leave now, you can still get six hours sleep.

GRAHAM: Cancel the three meetings. We're not leaving yet. I need truth and love more than I need sleep. I want to stay up half the night with our dear friends here. They've taught me something about time. It's similar to what Chesterton said about one of the silliest and most pervasive of all idolatries in our culture: that "you can't turn back the clock." He said, "Of course you can. And you must, if it's keeping bad time."

LEWIS AND TOLKIEN [together, spontaneously]: Good for you, Billy!

GRAHAM: Someone once criticized me for trying to turn back the clock a hundred years, and I replied that if I did that, I failed, because I was trying to turn it back two thousand years, to meet Jesus Christ in person. I think of the church as a time machine: It brings us back to Him.

TOLKIEN: We Catholics also think of the Church as a time machine, but we think she brings Him forward to us. That's the point of the sacraments.

GRAHAM: Again we find opposite roads to the same goal. All right, my friends, I'm here for another hour or so. Tollers, you gave me permission to dig at your innards, so here comes my shovel. It's made of questions.

TOLKIEN: All right, but why do you want to dig at *my* innards? I'm no more a holy man than I am a theologian.

GRAHAM: Because you're a good Catholic.

TOLKIEN: No, I'm not.

GRAHAM: You're not? What are you, then?

TOLKIEN: A bad Catholic. When I'm not struggling with despair, I'm struggling with pride or at least self-satisfaction. And, far worse, most of the time I'm not struggling at all.

GRAHAM: But you are a *believing* Catholic.

TOLKIEN: Yes.

GRAHAM: And a very thoughtful and imaginative one, if I may judge from your deservedly famous writings. But it's not because you're famous that I want to "pick at your innards", as you so elegantly put it, but because you're a Christian. One of us is importantly wrong about churches and sacraments, but neither of us is wrong about who our Lord and Savior is. I want to "dig at your innards" because, in the last analysis, I'm here in your house, not just to get to know you, but to know Him a little better. When I'm in your house and in your "innards" I'm in *His* house, because you *are* His house. I'm in church right now.

TOLKIEN: In one small room in it, even if it's only a tiny nursery room for one of His spiritual babies.

GRAHAM: And that is enough. For whenever I meet one of His children, I find different aspects of *Him*, many different reflections of God in His many different children. "Like Father, like son", they say. It's like seeing different reflections of the sun in the pieces of a broken mirror.

TOLKIEN: That's a beautiful image, Billy. All right, I'll try to help you satisfy that noble aspiration, even though I am quite certain ahead of time that I shall fail.

GRAHAM: And I am quite certain that you will succeed.

TOLKIEN: If so, it will not be because I am saintly but because you are.

GRAHAM: Neither of us is a saint, Tollers, but both of us are friends of Christ, and that's one reason why we should be friends of each other. And friends confide in each other.

TOLKIEN: Yes, of course, that's true, but you must realize, Billy, that Jack and I . . . well, we're just not very good at that sort of thing. We value friendships very highly, but it's usually confined to a few close ones. Jack and I are both very private persons. We're Brits, you know, not Americans, and that means that we're

. . . we're *proper*. We keep a stiff upper lip, and we wear a stiff collar to keep our chin up, and we don't talk much about ourselves and our feelings and what you like to call our personal relationship with God, as you and Guy do so easily. I'm not sure whether that's because you're Americans or because you're Protestants. Probably both.

GRAHAM: Perhaps it's because you're Stoics.

TOLKIEN: No, we're not Stoics. In fact, we're Romantics. Stoics disvalue their emotions, Romantics value them; that's why they put them into great poetry and not ordinary conversations.

But I shall try to stagger out of my snug and comfortable house and onto the open place that is quite familiar to you even though it's unfamiliar to me.

GRAHAM: I appreciate that, Tollers.

TOLKIEN: But I think I will need your permission to do something else first.

GRAHAM: What is that?

TOLKIEN: To refill my pipe, if you don't mind.

GRAHAM: Oh. Of course. Be my guest.

TOLKIEN: No, in my house you are my guest. You're not allergic to smoke?

GRAHAM: No. If I had been, I would have told you earlier.

TOLKIEN: Thanks. And does the same go for you, Guy?

GUY: Yes. Thanks for asking.

TOLKIEN: I need a few minutes to do three quick things, if you don't mind.

LEWIS: Take your time, Tollers. I have to go to the loo anyway.

GUY: The loo?

LEWIS: The W.C.

GUY: Sorry, I've not been in your country long enough . . .

LEWIS: We call it the water closet.

GUY: Oooh, so *that's* what that Frenchman meant when he asked, "Ou ay le dooble vay say?"

LEWIS: Your accent is abominable, but your deduction is good.

Tolkien gets up, refills his pipe, lights it [after a few attempts, with long-stemmed matches, not a lighter]. Then he goes to his bookcase and ruffles through a stack of papers, finally finding the one he wants. Then he goes into the kitchen and talks to Christopher for a minute, then returns, as does Lewis.

TOLKIEN: You ask me what the Eucharist means to me personally. Well, here is my answer in print. This is a letter I wrote to my son Michael. I've never shown it to anyone else. I think Michael was in his twenties at the time and he had just fallen in love, and he had written to me asking me about human love and marriage and romance and to what extent they can fulfill our hopes and desires. And my answer to him was this letter. Let's see, where is that paragraph? Oh, here it is:

Out of the darkness of my life, so much frustrated, I put before you the one great thing to love on earth: the Blessed Sacrament. . . . There you will find romance, glory, honour, fidelity, and the true way of all your loves on earth, and more than that: Death, by the divine paradox, that which ends life, and demands the surrender of all, and yet by the taste (or foretaste) of which alone can what you seek in your earthly relationships (love, faithfulness, joy) be maintained, or take on that complexion of reality, or eternal endurance, which every man's heart desires.[1]

Everyone is suddenly totally silent. It is a more sincere tribute than words.

GRAHAM: That's almost mystical.

TOLKIEN: But later I get practical:

The only cure for sagging faith is Communion. Though always Itself, perfect and complete and inviolate, the Blessed Sacrament does not operate completely and once for all in any of us. Like the act of Faith it must be continuous and grow by exercise. Frequency is of the highest effect. Seven times a week is more nourishing than seven times at intervals. Also I can recommend this as an exercise . . . : make your communion in circumstances that affront your taste. Choose a snuffling or gabbling priest or a proud and

---

[1] It has been shared with a few million more people since Tolkien's death because it has been published in *The Letters of J. R. R. Tolkien* (New York: Houghton Mifflin Harcourt, 2000), pp. 53–54.

vulgar friar; and a church full of the usual bour-
geois crowd, ill-behaved children—from those
who yell to those products of Catholic schools
who the moment the tabernacle is opened sit
back and yawn—open necked and dirty youths,
women in trousers and often with hair both un-
kempt and uncovered. Go to Communion *with*
them (and pray for them). It will be just the
same (or better than that) as a mass said beau-
tifully by a visibly holy man, and shared by a
few devout and decorous people. (It could not
be worse than the mess of the feeding of the
Five Thousand—after which [Our] Lord pro-
pounded the feeding that was to come.)[2]

GRAHAM: "The feeding that was to come"—do you
mean the Eucharist?

TOLKIEN: Yes. What came next was His scandalous
discourse on the Eucharist, after which most of His
disciples left Him. That came right after the feeding
of the five thousand in John's Gospel, chapter six. It
was His commentary on the miracle that He had just
finished. The feeding of the five thousand had only
been a symbol of the feeding that was to come. It
was the greater miracle that the lesser miracle symbolized.

GRAHAM: I like very much that last bit in your letter, Tollers, about mingling with ordinary people, as
Jesus did, rather than finding some nice, clean aes-
thetic refuge from them. And I am struck by the jux-

---

[2] Ibid., pp. 338–39.

taposition you make between the Sacrament and the people. I always focused on the people rather than on the sacraments, and I thought you Catholics focused too much on the sacraments rather than the people, but you put the two together.

TOLKIEN: And that's exactly what Jack does, too, in something he wrote about the Sacrament. May I read that to you, too?

GRAHAM: Can you hold onto that for a few minutes? I'd like to talk about your quotation first, if you don't mind.

TOLKIEN: Aha, you are onto me, Billy. I can't divert your focus away from me and onto Jack, as Saint Peter tried to divert Christ's focus onto John.

GRAHAM: You mean that scene on the beach?

TOLKIEN: Yes, after the Resurrection. Peter had said to Our Lord, just before His capture and trial, that even if everyone else forsook Him, he never would; and then Peter had denied Him three times. So when Christ asked Peter three times if he loved Him, he was upset, and after the third question, Peter said, "What about this man, Lord?" He was trying to distract Jesus' gaze to John, the only disciple who showed his love in action by staying with Him even to the end.

GRAHAM: You know your Bible, Tollers. I didn't think Catholics usually did.

TOLKIEN: We're catching up to you there, even if you're not catching up to us yet in the sacraments.

GRAHAM: You say, "the only cure for lagging faith is frequent Communion." I'd say the only cure is frequent Bible reading.

TOLKIEN: It's the same Person we meet in both.

GRAHAM: I agree.

TOLKIEN: But we meet only His mind in the Bible, while we meet His whole person, body and soul, in the Sacrament.

GRAHAM: Well, we also meet His Body in His people.

TOLKIEN: That's true, too, isn't it? Yes, in the Bible both the Sacrament and the Church are called "the Body of Christ". Saint Augustine says that we become the Body of Christ (the Church) when we receive the Body of Christ (the Sacrament).

GRAHAM: But the "Body of Christ" is first of all His people.

TOLKIEN: No, I think it's first of all the Eucharist. The people are defined by the Eucharist; the Eucharist is not defined by the people. The Eucharist, not the people, is the standard, the perfection that judges the imperfection and saves it. His people are sinners; His Sacrament is sinless.

GRAHAM: I understand what you believe there, I think, and I respect your motives for believing it, even though I don't share your sacramental theology and don't *worship* the Eucharist. But all of those things that you say you find in the Blessed Sacrament—love and honor and fidelity and immortality—I find exactly the same thing in the same Christ. But I find

Christ mediated to me through the Bible, first of all, and I believe in the sacraments and in the church only because I find them in the Bible.

TOLKIEN: Augustine would say you have it backwards. He wrote, "I would not believe in the Scriptures if it were not for the authority of the Church."

GRAHAM: Well, good Christians, and even the saints, can disagree about important things.

TOLKIEN: They can, and they do, but they shouldn't. At least not if we take Saint Paul seriously when he told the Corinthians he had zero tolerance for denominationalism. Remember? "One says, I follow Paul, and one says, I follow Apollos."

GRAHAM: Once again I totally agree. Disunity is a terrible tragedy.

TOLKIEN: But—to be so candid as to be impolite— *we* didn't create it. You did. You tore the seamless garment. We tried to hold it together.

GUY: We're descending into polemics now.

TOLKIEN: Sorry. You're right. We're supposed to be focusing on the Eucharist and Eucharistic devotion. All right, here, I think it's time for me to share with you one other quotation about what the Eucharist means to us Catholics, Anglican as well as Roman.

GRAHAM: What saint is it from?

TOLKIEN [laughing]: It's from Jack, here, who is too saintly and humble to put it forward himself.

LEWIS: You see, Billy, we're both quite proud of each other's humility.

TOLKIEN [ignoring the interruption]: It tells you what the Eucharist means to *him*, and it's the same as what it means to me, and that's what you want to know, right?

GRAHAM: Right.

TOLKIEN: I declare unequivocally that this is the best paragraph he has ever written in any of his dozens of books and hundreds of articles and thousands of letters. It's from a sermon he preached at the Magdalen College chapel. He entitled it "The Weight of Glory". It may not seem to be about the Eucharist except in the very last sentence, but it is, and it shows what difference our faith in the Eucharist makes in our daily lives. I think that's what you want to know, right?

GRAHAM: Right.

TOLKIEN: It's the very heart of what you might call a typically Catholic sacramental sensibility like Jack's. And mine, too, though I'm not nearly so eloquent. Here is the conclusion to Jack's sermon:

> It is a serious thing to live in a society of possible gods and goddesses, to remember that the dullest and most uninteresting person you talk to may one day be a creature which, if you saw it now, you would be strongly tempted to worship, or else a horror and a corruption such as you now meet, if at all, only in a nightmare. All day long we are, in some degree, helping each

other to one or other of these destinations. It is in the light of these overwhelming possibilities, it is with the awe and circumspection proper to them, that we should conduct all our dealings with one another, all friendships, all loves, all play, all politics. There are no *ordinary* people. You have never talked to a mere mortal. Nations, cultures, arts, civilization—these are mortal, and their life is to ours as the life of a gnat. But it is immortals whom we joke with, work with, marry, snub, and exploit—immortal horrors or everlasting splendours. This does not mean that we are to be perpetually solemn. We must play. But our merriment must be of that kind (and it is, in fact, the merriest kind) which exists between people who have, from the outset, taken each other seriously—no flippancy, no superiority, no presumption. And our charity must be a real and costly love, with deep feeling for the sins in spite of which we love the sinner —no mere tolerance or indulgence which parodies love as flippancy parodies merriment. Next to the Blessed Sacrament itself, your neighbor is the holiest object presented to your senses. If he is your Christian neighbor he is holy in almost the same way, for in him also Christ *vere latitat* —the glorifier and the glorified, Glory Himself, is truly hidden.[3]

There is silence for a full ten seconds, like the silence after Holy Communion itself.

---

[3] C. S. Lewis, *The Weight of Glory* (New York: HarperCollins, 2001), pp. 46–47.

GRAHAM: That is profoundly true, and life-changing, and it is exactly the conclusion I get from what the Bible says. Christ hides in His children. I think there are more similarities between your Eucharist-centered devotion and my Bible-centered devotion than either of us thought.

TOLKIEN: I see the deep agreement about Christ hiding in persons, but I also see a deep disagreement about whether He is hiding in the Eucharist. It's the difference between a picture and a person. Is the Eucharist a picture of Christ or the Person of Christ? A symbol or the substance?

GRAHAM: And I, too, see the deep difference, but I also see the deep similarity.

TOLKIEN: I am a little reluctant to say any more, though there is much more to say.

GRAHAM: Why?

TOLKIEN: Because I am not a theologian.

GRAHAM: I didn't come here to listen to your theology. I came here to listen to your heart and to your faith.

TOLKIEN: But my faith comes from my theology.

GRAHAM: But I'm here to hear what difference it makes to your heart and your life.

TOLKIEN: I will tell you. It is a blood transfusion. It is the exact reverse of Dracula.

GRAHAM: Dracula?

TOLKIEN: Yes. Dracula is like the devil, or like the Antichrist. He takes your blood, your life, your identity, out of you and into himself. So you lose your humanity, forever. Christ is the opposite of the Antichrist. He gives you His blood, His life, He shares His very identity with you, so that Saint Paul can say: "I live, nevertheless not I but Christ lives in me."

GRAHAM: I believe that, too, but I think that happens by faith.

TOLKIEN: It begins there, but it doesn't end there.

GRAHAM: You mean we also have to do good works?

TOLKIEN: Yes, but that's not what I mean. I wasn't thinking of what we do but of what He does. Our faith accepts His gift, but the sacraments *are* His gifts. And we need them because we can't climb that mountain, but He can come down. We can't make ourselves divine, but He can make Himself human. The sacraments are extensions of the Incarnation.

GRAHAM: I am learning something new here. I had thought you Catholics were stuck in a kind of works-righteousness, but now I think I'm seeing the opposite in you. It's all grace.

TOLKIEN: That's what one of the saints said on her deathbed.

GRAHAM: But for me it's faith, not sacraments, that receives His grace. Sacraments only *express* our faith.

TOLKIEN: Well, they do, because if we didn't have faith, we wouldn't go to receive the sacraments. But it's more than that: it's our body, our mouth, that receives the Eucharist. We are like infants at the breast.

GRAHAM: I see. For you it is very physical.

TOLKIEN: Yes. It's spiritual, too. It's not either/or.

GRAHAM: And very literal.

TOLKIEN: Yes, and symbolic, too. That also is not an either/or. So are the Cross and the Resurrection very symbolic as well as very literal. It's in many of the pre-Christian myths, symbolically, but not literally, not historically. Jack wrote an essay once entitled "Myth Become Fact". As God becomes Man, as eternity becomes time, as the eternal *logos*, the eternal truth, becomes historical, so the myth becomes fact, the symbol becomes substance, without ceasing to be a symbol, as God becomes Man without ceasing to be God.

GRAHAM: I think I understand those categories. But can you put it into personal terms? How do you translate that theology into experience, that literalness into life? Just how literal is it for you?

TOLKIEN: Here's an example. I read this story in the papers. There was an earthquake in Armenia that buried a young mother and her three-year-old daughter for eight days. When the rescuers dug them out, they found the child alive because the mother had cut her hand and let her daughter drink her blood. She died, and the child was saved. The Eucharist is that literal for me.

There's another story, about a small boy whose sister needed a blood transfusion to survive, but the only person they could find who had her rare blood type was her little brother. He volunteered to give her a blood transfusion, and after a few minutes on the table he asked the nurse, "How soon will I die?" You see, that's what He said: "This is my blood, shed for you."

GRAHAM: How literal it is for you!

TOLKIEN: How literal He is! He is literal, and the Cross is literal, and so is the Sacrament. It's as literal as the Cross is literal. The blood that saves the world is His literal Blood.

The Jews said, "If you come down from the cross, we will believe in you." If he had come down from the Cross without shedding His blood, He would have won their faith and their allegiance, but not their salvation. He would not have saved them because He would not have given them His blood.

You ask me what the Eucharist means to me, and I will reply by quoting a famous atheist and materialist, Ludwig Feuerbach. He had no idea that his most famous saying is really the explanation for the Eucharist. In German, the saying goes "Man ist was er isst." In English, it's "You are what you eat." Those five words: that's what the Eucharist is to me: my identity. My destined identity, not my achieved identity. I'm not Saint Paul, so I can't yet honestly say, "I live, yet I no longer live, but it's Christ, not me, who lives in me." But that is what I will say after I die, God willing. Saint Augustine also said the same thing in four words: "Become what you consume." And in another place, he says, "You are the Body of Christ; this is the Body of Christ; and by doing this you become what you are, the Body of Christ." So if you ask me what the Eucharist is to me, I have to say that it is not only my joy in this world and my hope for the next, but also that it is my *identity*. If when

I died I somehow discovered that it was all a lie, I think I could no longer be me, I would no longer have any meaning left to the word "I".

Austin Farrer, who is an Anglican and a very good friend of both Jack and myself, once said that "The Holy Communion is not a special part of our religion; it is our religion, sacramentally enacted." The Real Presence means that it doesn't merely symbolize Christ, it is Christ. When the priest holds Him in his hands, he holds Him who holds him in His hands. When we consume Him, we let Him consume us.

GRAHAM: That sounds very mystical.

TOLKIEN: It is. It is very mystical *and* very literal. Literal things are far more mystical than mere ideas. I have often thought that one of the most mystical of all things is a tree. Especially the one that was made into a Cross and that held Christ.

GRAHAM: How do you get from that to the social dimension, to living a life of charity?

TOLKIEN: There's no distance. It's essentially social. Augustine shows that when he writes this. [He shuffles some papers, finds it, and reads:] "You are the Body of Christ. That is to say, in you and through you the work of the Incarnation must go forward." And then, to show that he means more than just prayer and worship and "the imitation of Christ" morally, he says, "You are to be taken, consecrated, broken, and distributed, that you may be the means of grace and vehicles of Eternal Charity." That's what Jack meant in that quotation from "The Weight of Glory".

GRAHAM: That is mystical, too.

TOLKIEN: It sounds as if you are accusing it rather than praising it.

GRAHAM: I am ambivalent. I tend to be a bit suspicious of mysticism.

TOLKIEN: Why?

GRAHAM: For one thing, I don't find it in the Bible. All of Scripture's descriptions of heavenly worship are public, not private.

TOLKIEN: It's both.

GRAHAM: To you.

TOLKIEN: No, to Scripture.

GRAHAM: Where?

TOLKIEN: Well, one of my favorite passages in Scripture that I think one would have to call "mystical" is when Our Lord knocks Saul of Tarsus off his high horse first physically and then spiritually when He says, "Saul, Saul, why do you persecute me?" Saul has been persecuting *Christians*, not Christ. He thinks Christ is dead. He knows this is the voice of God, so he asks, in utter confusion, "Who are you, Lord?" He is in shock. His question shows that he now knows he has gotten God wrong—the God that was his whole life. And Our Lord replies, "I am Jesus, whom you are persecuting." And that was an absolute smackdown shock. And it's a double shock to Saul: the identity of Christ with God and the identity of Christ with Christians, with Christ's Church, which in Scripture has the same name as the Eucharist, namely, "the Body of Christ".

GRAHAM: That is indeed Scripture, and it is indeed a very high view of Christians. We are the Body of Christ!

TOLKIEN: High, yes, but not flattering. I have another quote—here it is—that defines the Eucharist by these words: the Eucharist is "Jesus Christ handed over into the hands of sinners".

And here's another one, and it also shocks you and stretches you incredibly: "I eat God, and I have His life in me. It's the best thing in the world. But you have to die to yourself."

GRAHAM: I'm impressed, but I can't help still feeling it's too materialistic.

TOLKIEN: If Jesus walked into this room, how would you respond?

GRAHAM: As John did in Revelation. I'd fall at His feet as one dead.

TOLKIEN: You know Him well, Billy. Now is that a physical act?

GRAHAM: Yes.

TOLKIEN: You Protestants put the words of Scripture first. But I think you really know better than that in your hearts. I think if Jesus showed up here, it would be a long time before you got to words.

GRAHAM: I see. That's why you are silent after Communion.

TOLKIEN: Yes.

GRAHAM: So you actually believe you eat Him.

TOLKIEN: Yes. We eat the meaning of life. We eat the way and the truth and the life.

GRAHAM: Wouldn't a theologian say you are confusing holy abstractions with a holy Person?

TOLKIEN: A good theologian would not. Saint Paul would not. In 1 Corinthians (1:30) he said that God has made Him to *be* our wisdom, our righteousness, our sanctification, and our redemption. He said not only that Christ *gave* us wisdom and righteousness and sanctification and redemption but that He *is* those four things. He was not reducing Christ to those four things; he was reducing those four things to Christ. Christ Himself did the same thing when He said, "I am the way, and the truth, and the life." Not "I teach the way, the truth, and the life", but "I AM the way, and the truth, and the life." That is indeed, as you say, very mystical. And also very personal. And very concrete, not abstract.

GRAHAM: It's astounding. I believe that, too. We Evangelicals have always focused on the very Person of Christ, not on abstractions or concepts, however important they may be. I see now that we are both profoundly Christocentric. That was my main fear: that you were worshipping something else in addition to Christ: sacraments, rules, organizations, churches, saints, relics, popes, Mary, whatever. Now I see a precious and simple point. I don't know about all those other issues, but I know that in your mind you are not an idolater of the Eucharist because you believe the Eucharist IS Christ.

LEWIS: As Aslan is Christ.

GRAHAM: Yes. I remember those letters from children that you told us about and your answer to them, Jack. Not Aslan instead of Christ but Aslan IS Christ.

LEWIS: But of course Aslan is a fiction, but the Eucharist is a fact.

GRAHAM: I think your sacramental theology is as fictional as Aslan, but I think your heart is in love with the real Lion—"the Lion of the Tribe of Judah". Wherever you believe Christ is, that's where you want to be. [Lewis and Tolkien both nod.]

I want that, too. That's why I came here today. My Bible tells me that He promised that if two or three are gathered in His name, He will be really present in the midst of them.

TOLKIEN: So you agree with my heart but not my head.

GRAHAM: Yes.

TOLKIEN: That's terribly important, of course. But do you think the heart can substitute for the head?

GRAHAM: No, but it can go first. Orthopraxy teaching orthodoxy. The heart sends blood to the brain. The heart motivates the mind.

TOLKIEN: And do you say that the heart can have reasons that the reason cannot know, as Pascal says?

GRAHAM: I think so.

TOLKIEN: I'm suspicious of that. The role of the heart isn't to think.

GRAHAM: You don't think there's an eye in the heart?

TOLKIEN: No. If there were, we wouldn't need a mind too.

GRAHAM: Let me ask you a question. If Guy were a great psychologist and he knew you even better than Jack did, but Jack loved you more than Guy did, wouldn't you say Jack's eye of the heart understands you better than Guy does?

TOLKIEN: Oh, yes, of course. I'd explain that in different terms—I wouldn't say the heart itself has an eye—but I admit the fact. In fact, I celebrate it.

GRAHAM: Then the love in the heart can teach the mind.

TOLKIEN: Yes.

GRAHAM: But teachers have to see something if they are going to teach it.

TOLKIEN: Yes.

GRAHAM: Then there is an eye in the heart.

TOLKIEN: *Quod erat demonstrandum!* I didn't know you were a debater, Billy.

GRAHAM [laughing]: Neither did I. I think I must be catching the disease from the two of you. Oxford is notorious for it, but I didn't think the infection could be caught so easily.

Seriously, Tollers, I'm very grateful to you for coming out of your British suit of armor to me. You did that with your heart, and your heart has taught my mind something, I think.

TOLKIEN: About my theology?

GRAHAM: No, about your faith.

TOLKIEN: But neither of us has budged an inch in our faith. We've come closer as friends, yes, but not as theologians. What has this "eye of the heart" actually taught our heads about the issue, about the objective truth?

GRAHAM: Let me try an experiment to answer that question. Try to formulate our difference about the Eucharist as sharply as you can, show me the biggest divide between us, and I'll try to show you what bridge I see over it.

TOLKIEN: Fine. You want something simple and sharp and clear and concrete, right?

GRAHAM: Yes. And something from you, not just quoted from your catechism.

TOLKIEN: Fine. Here it is. Imagine Jesus Christ is standing here before you, really here, just as literally as He was two thousand years ago, twenty feet in front of you. Let's say it's His Second Coming. He has descended from Heaven and landed directly in front of you, and He is about to judge you and take you to Heaven with Him. He smiles at you and tells you He loves you, in spite of all your stupid, silly, shallow, selfish sins. He shows you the scars on His hands and feet, as he did to "Doubting Thomas". What do you do? What do you say?

GRAHAM: I would say exactly what Thomas did: I would say, "My Lord and my God!", and I would fall down at His feet and worship Him.

TOLKIEN: Good. Now imagine that after you do that, He holds up a six-foot-high piece of plywood in front of Him like a shield and stands behind it. You can no longer see Him, but you know He is there. How does that change your reaction to Him?

GRAHAM: It doesn't. I would say and do the same thing.

TOLKIEN: Well, that's what you *would* do, but that's what I *do* do.

GRAHAM [stunned]: Oh.

TOLKIEN: I am glad to hear your "Oh". Now you see why I say there is a large and heavy difference between us.

GRAHAM: You misunderstand. I said "Oh" because now I see that the difference between us is as small and thin as plywood.

TOLKIEN: Oh. I think it is now my turn to utter that sacred syllable.

GRAHAM: Did you notice that the very thing that made the difference between us so great was the thing that made it small?

TOLKIEN: That is quite a paradox. What do you mean?

GRAHAM: What seems to make the difference between us so great? Why did it seem to be a black or white either/or? It was Jack's argument that the issue of the Real Presence is an either/or that is very similar to the "Lord, Liar, or Lunatic" argument about Christ's claim to divinity.

TOLKIEN: Yes. Both arguments leave no room for compromise, no middle position. How do you see that as narrowing our gap, or bridging it? It does the opposite.

GRAHAM: It also unites us. Because your love of Our Lord with your whole heart and soul and mind and strength is the whole reason why you bow down, why you fall on the Catholic side of the line that divides us. And that very same love in me is the whole reason why I fall on the Protestant side. It's the very same reason: it's the very same Lord.

TOLKIEN: Oh.

No one speaks. All spontaneously nod and silently pray.

12

Conclusions?

GUY [after a pause]: Gentlemen, I regret to say that we need to be leaving. However relative time may be to the soul, Billy's body is still in material time and needs at least a little rest. It has been a great pleasure and a great privilege for us.

LEWIS [to Graham]: Billy, tell me honestly: Are you disappointed with what we've done or not done today? Did you hope to find or hear or say or do something other than what you found or heard or did or said?

GRAHAM: On the contrary, I am exhilarated. I am thrilled to have been among the giants on the earth.

LEWIS: I think you are confusing hobbits with giants. But I don't mean my question personally, about your feelings toward us, but about your faith. Did we help you to see anything better, to see any more light?

GRAHAM: Of course.

LEWIS: How did we do that?

GRAHAM: You helped me come a little closer to the Light of the World, even if that was not your conscious intention. And how could you *not* do that?

When committed Christians talk seriously together, it is like iron sharpening iron, as Scripture says.

LEWIS: But no one changed his mind, no one convinced anyone else that his position was true, and we are still as far apart as we were at the beginning, aren't we? (I am playing devil's advocate here, of course.)

GRAHAM: Not so. Get thee behind me, Satan, you are a liar. I for one have made very significant progress, I think, in understanding views I did not understand before, and your reasons for them, and in admiring your motives and your loves and seeing how similar they are to mine, even though I do not agree with your theology.

LEWIS: But—just to try to make a useful pest of myself by continuing to play devil's advocate—isn't it true that that was almost inevitable? As you say, whenever committed Christians talk seriously, iron sharpens iron.

GRAHAM: Yes, but I think the *amount* of sharpening was remarkable, not inevitable. And I am more hopeful about ecumenism now that I have met you than I was before, even though the gap between us has become clearer and sharper and therefore apparently greater.

GUY: That sounds like a contradiction.

LEWIS: Not if the closeness as well as the farness has become clearer and sharper.

GRAHAM: I am impressed and grateful to you, Jack, and to you, too, Tollers, for carving out a place for us in your house and a time for us in your life. It was pure grace.

TOLKIEN: No, it was grace plus good works.

GUY [not comprehending that Tolkien is trying to make a joke]: I, too, thank you for your good works, Tollers, but I don't expect God to thank me for mine. When I show up at the golden gates I'm not going to pull out two tickets, just one.

LEWIS: What do you mean by two tickets? There's only one Christ for all four of us.

GUY: But you say there are two connections with Him: faith and good works, or faith and sacraments (assuming sacraments *are* good works). The faith ticket is the only one I'm going to carry. When they ask me for my ticket, I'm not going to talk about the sacraments, I'm just going to say, "I'm only a sinner, saved by grace."

LEWIS: Oh, so am I. The sacraments are pure grace. They're not our works; they're God's.

TOLKIEN: Remember the words of Saint Thérèse: "*Everything* is a grace."

GUY: What about nature?

TOLKIEN: Our friend Charles Williams said that "nature is the nature of grace."

GRAHAM: That's beautiful, but please, no more theological arguments!

We haven't changed our minds theologically, and yet I think we have all changed our minds about each other personally and arrived at a kind of mountain-top, coming up three or four very different roads. They remain just as different as they ever were, but they've brought us to the same top, a sort of Mount of Transfiguration. So I don't think we can go any farther in that direction, unless we learn to fly.

LEWIS: May I make a proposal? The sun has gone down hours ago, so I think the time has come for us to imitate it and go down, too, down our separate roads from that summit, like the enlightened prisoner who has climbed out of Plato's cave and then goes back down into the cave to try to share the light with the other prisoners.

GRAHAM: You mean sharing our ecumenical passion with other Christians.

LEWIS: Yes, but also something more literal: leaving the mountaintop of Tollers' house and hospitality. Tollers, I think you must have some Elvish blood in you; how else could you write so convincingly about Elves? And how else could you live in a real place that feels so much like Rivendell?

TOLKIEN: The pleasure was mine.

GRAHAM AND GUY [together]: And ours.

They shake hands and leave, but the handshakes as well as the headshakes remain in their hearts.